THE COMPLETE GUIDE TO THE MUSIC OF

3 1705 00402 6115

DEDICATION & ACKNOWLEDGEMENTS

For Sean Russell Hogan (1964-1993) and Roman Henning Martin (1993–)

Strange days found me while I was writing this book. Thanks are due first and foremost to Ellie, for being her wonderful self, and for holding my hand as we walked through the Valley of the Shadow. I'd also like to thank Chris Charlesworth, Patrick Humphries, Frank Wynne and Charles Shaar Murray, basically just for being damn fine chaps. No thanks at all are due to the Allied Irish Bank or UFO Records.

Peter K Hogan, London, '93

BY PETER K HOGAN

Copyright © 1994 Omnibus Press (A Division of Book Sales Limited)

Edited by Chris Charlesworth
Cover & Book designed by 4i Limited
Picture research by David Brolan

ISBN: 0.7119.3527.0 Order No: OP47342

Exclusive Distributors
Book Sales Limited, 8/9 Frith Street, London W1V 5TZ, UK.
Music Sales Corporation, 257 Park Avenue South, New York, NY 10010, USA.
Music Sales Pty Limited, 120 Rothschild Avenue, Rosebery, NSW 2018, Australia.

To the Music Trade only:
Music Sales Limited, 8/9, Frith Street, London W1V 5TZ, UK.

Photo credits: London Features International: 15, 60, 97, 106t, 107 insets,109r&br, 110 x 4, 112;
Barry Plummer: vi, 10, 41, 110; Pictorial Press: iv, 5, 20, 47, 91, 106b, 108;
Gloria Stavers/Star File: front cover, ii, 23, 79, 100, 107.
Every effort has been made to trace the copyright holders of the photographs in this book but one or
two were unreachable. We would be grateful if the photographers concerned would contact us.

Printed in the United Kingdom by Ebenezer Baylis Limited, Worcester

A catalogue record for this book is available from the British Library.

OMNIBUS PRESS
LONDON · NEW YORK · SYDNEY

Contents

Introduction

A lot has been written and said about the 1960s, and most of it is clichéd bollocks. It is true that it was a time of genuine experimentation and innovation in the popular arts, and that nearly all of these cultural movers and shakers were _unbelievably_ young. But it's also a fact that that era can never be reconstructed (no matter how many times the fashions and the music get recycled) – and that's definitely a good thing, 'cause it wasn't _all_ unbridled fun and excitement.

In this post Geldof world, it's hard to convey to anybody who didn't go through it that a mere 25 years ago you could be (in my case, often) sworn and spat at in the street, just because of the way you looked and dressed; hard to get across the liberating feeling that every social change, no matter how small, was a genuine revolution against the rigid thinking of one's parents – maybe even the beginning of a new world (which it actually was; it just wasn't the world we hoped for). Or the anguish (and fear) that sprang from knowing that thousands of your contemporaries were dying in a futile and dishonest war in S.E. Asia, where the spectre of escalation to nukes seemed an ever-present threat (Richard Nixon was in favour of it), Or the disappointment in discovering that LSD was not going to save the world after all, but was (a) damn dangerous (b) spiritually fraudulent and (c) in all probability a CIA-controlled social experiment.

Against this social and political backdrop, a thousand rock bands had emerged in the wake of The Beatles and Dylan, all of them with something to say about the state of the world. But The Doors stood apart from most of the herd – there were obviously influences at play in their music other than

the usual blues riffs and hippie clichés; they were harder edged, had more in common with New York's Velvet Underground than with their West Coast contemporaries. They were just different.

And the difference was largely due to their singer, Jim Morrison. That's not to denigrate the input of the other Doors – their backing was a perfect channel for Morrison's vision, and a sound unlike any other (at the time), that made you sit up and pay attention. But the vision itself – the words, the image, the politics, the whole approach – belonged (mainly if not exclusively) to Jim.

Morrison was a talented singer and lyricist; he was also a poet, an artist, a film-maker and an "erotic politician", with a reported I.Q. of 149. On the downside, even his defenders admit that he was often the kind of person you'd cross the street to avoid: boorish, rude, unreliable, antagonistic, usually abusing at least one variety of substance and quite possibly dangerous. Yet according to one person who worked in The Doors' office, "98% of the time Jim was a gentleman".

For many listeners, The Doors were the first band to uncover the true potential of rock; the revelation that a pop song needn't be mindless doggerel caused many converts to go over the top (Joan Didion called The Doors "the Norman Mailers of the Top 40, missionaries of apocalyptic sex"). Listening to their music now, and being as dispassionate and harsh as possible, I'd say about half of their output still stands up well – but that's a lot more than I could say for most of their contemporaries (leaving out the nostalgia factor).

Art aside, Morrison himself had no doubts as to the core of their popularity: "We appeal to the same human needs as classical tragedy and early Southern blues. Think of it as a séance in an environment which has become hostile to life; cold, restrictive. People feel they're dying in a bad landscape. So they gather together in a séance in order to invoke, palliate, and drive away the dead through chanting, singing, dancing and music. They try to cure an illness, to bring back harmony into the world."

Jim was a reluctant rock star, who hated his teenage fans. For him, the only reason to perform was to push the envelope, to see how far he could go with an audience; there's no doubt at all that he did truly see himself as a shaman, releasing the energy of a concert crowd to cathartic effect (on the audience and himself). "There are no rules at a rock concert," he proclaimed joyfully. "Anything is possible."

And Morrison wasn't just crying shaman – he really meant it: "Sometimes I like to look at the history of rock'n'roll like the origin of Greek drama, which started out on a threshing floor at the crucial seasons and was originally a band of worshippers, dancing and singing. Then, one day a possessed person jumped out of the crowd and started imitating a god."

If he was imitating a god, it must have been Dionysus; if he was a fool, he was a holy fool. He had, as Gene Sculatti observed in Cool: A Hipster's Directory (Vermilion, 1982) "the courage to make a fool of himself, often and in public". Like William Blake, Morrison believed that "the road of excess leads to the palace of wisdom"; unfortunately, he took that saying to heart in his personal life as well as in his art.

And nothing exceeds like excess: Jim would routinely drink enough to put most people in hospital; strangers would come up to him in the street and give him pills which he'd swallow without even bothering to ask what they were. As a motorist he'd drive the wrong way down one-way streets at sixty miles per hour; as a pedestrian, he'd always wait until the lights changed and traffic was moving towards him before attempting to cross a road. Self-destructive? Certainly. A death wish? That's too simple, too glib. Nor was Morrison's lifestyle a simple search for adventure... it was closer to exploration, as he put it himself in 1969: "Let's just say I was testing the bounds of reality. I was curious to see what would happen. That's all it was: just curiosity."

But he was without doubt also a hedonist, and then some - perhaps at least partly because he was so nihilistic in his view of life and society ("I wanna have my kicks before the whole shithouse goes up in flames," he observes on one of the live tapes). And while Blake's comment about the road of excess definitely carries a seed of truth, it's also true that that road quite often leads to the graveyard as well (or instead). Jim Morrison lived fast and died young... but the corpse he left behind was not good looking, nor was it even in remotely good shape.

Had he lived, he might have returned to the studio one day, perhaps even survived the passing decades with as much dignity as Van Morrison or Dylan. Or not - we'll never know. But he was a genuine one-off, and ahead of his time; and his nihilism had its positive side too, more easily recognisable in these days of chaos culture : "I am interested in anything about revolt, disorder, chaos, especially activity that seems to have no meaning. It seems to me to be the road to freedom." Those words could just as easily have been said by Brian Eno, or David Byrne, or David Bowie (or Richard Feynman, for that matter).

That he has become a greater icon in death than he was in life is something that would probably have amused him greatly. As he wrote in one of his notebooks, "I contend an abiding sense of irony over all I do."

Peter K Hogan, October, 1993

the Opening of the Doors

"They claim everyone was born, but I don't recall it. Maybe I was having one of my blackouts." – Jim Morrison, 1969.

James Douglas Morrison was born on December 8, 1943, in Melbourne, Florida. His mother, Clara, had met newly-graduated naval officer George S. Morrison (known as 'Steve') at a Navy dance in late 1941, when she was just 21; the bombing of Pearl Harbour occurred shortly afterwards, and it seemed certain that Steve would soon see active duty. The couple married in April 1942, and Steve shipped out for the North Pacific almost immediately. The following year he returned to the States, and the couple travelled to Florida, where Steve was to undergo flight training. Eleven months later, Jim was born. The Morrisons would have two more children, Ann and Andrew, who were respectively three and six years younger than Jim.

At the age of about four or five, Jim was driving with his parents and grandparents somewhere in the Southwest when they passed a car crash – a truckload of Indian workers had struck another car, and several bodies lay in the road, literally bleeding to death. Morrison would relate years later that this was his first experience of death, and – as there was little they could do to help – of his parents' fallibility. And something happened to Jim then, as he told Frank Lisciandro: "And like, this is a projection from a long way back, but I do think that, at that moment, the soul or the ghosts of those dead Indians, maybe one or two of 'em, were running around freaking out, and just leaped into my soul, and I was like a sponge, ready to just sit there and absorb it... it's not a ghost story, it's something that really means something to me."

Like most military families, the Morrisons travelled around a lot. Jim grew up in Alexandra, Virginia; Clearwater, Florida; Washington D.C.; Albuquerque, New Mexico; Claremont and Alameda, California; and three or four other places. Steve Morrison was away for long periods of time (when Jim was six months old, Steve went off to war; he didn't see his young son again for three years); he saw duty in Korea, and eventually rose through the ranks to become a Rear Admiral. So Jim grew up without a father most of the time, and this may well be the key to understanding his wayward psyche. Perhaps because he blamed his father for the way he was raised, or perhaps simply because he despised his father's profession (having a father who was a high-ranking officer in the armed services during the Vietnam War wasn't exactly the kind of thing you bragged about), Jim Morrison would consistently claim in early interviews that both his parents were dead. "I just didn't want to involve them," he explained in 1969. "I guess I said it as a kind of a joke – it's easy enough to find out the personal details if you really want to..."

But if Jim grew up rootless, he was also popular and athletic, renowned for a weird sense of humour and practical jokes. He was a bit of a daredevil, and a bit of a rebel, and he hungered for word of others like himself. He read everything he could lay his hands on, from *Mad* magazine to the beat poets and beyond: Blake, Kerouac, Colin Wilson, Celine, Sartre, Rimbaud, Aldous Huxley, Ginsberg, Balzac, Cocteau, Joyce... anything that came to hand. If there was a record on Jim's turntable, it was as likely to be Lawrence Ferlinghetti reciting his poetry as Elvis Presley reciting his. During this period Morrison also discovered the works of Friedrich Nietzsche, and found in the German philosopher a voice he could understand and relate to (just check out the Oedipal section of *The Birth Of Tragedy*).

But all this highbrow stuff may not have been the *biggest* influence on the young Jim, as he recalled in 1968: "I grew up with Elvis Presley, Frankie Avalon, Fabian, all those guys. They were all making a social comment; their being was a social comment." He'd already tried learning the piano, but "didn't have the discipline to keep it up".

When Jim was 15, the family moved to Washington, where they stayed for three years while Jim attended George Washington High School. Although he'd dabbled with poetry before, at this point Jim got serious about it ('Horse Latitudes' was written during this period), writing incessantly in a series of journals and notebooks. "When I left school, for some dumb reason – or maybe it was wise – I threw all those books away, and there's nothing I can think of that I'd rather have in my possession now than those lost books," he later said, but conceded, "maybe if I'd never thrown them away, I'd never have written anything original, 'cause they were mainly things that I had hoard or read, like quotes from books... I think if I'd never got rid of them, I'd never have freed myself."

His father was rarely present, and he shared little rapport with Jim when he was; Clara simply nagged him constantly, about his hair, appearance and all the usual adolescent stuff. Jim escaped as often as he could, to downtown Washington to listen to blues bands in sleazy bars. He graduated from George Washington High School in 1961, though his parents thought him lazy (he got good grades without really trying). Steve and Clara then enrolled him in St Petersburg Junior College in Florida, and sent him to spend a year living in Clearwater, Florida with his grandparents. Jim quickly discovered that getting drunk and generally pursuing the Bohemian life annoyed the hell out of his grandparents, so he did both with a vengeance. When the year was up, Jim began classes at Florida State University – "mainly because I couldn't think of anything else to do," as he later put it. He studied (among other things) philosophy and crowd psychology, where he doubtless picked up a few tricks he'd use later on in life. But he wanted to leave, to study cinematography at UCLA. Unable to persuade his parents to agree to this, he enrolled in as many theatre-related classes at Florida

State as possible. He was still determined to get to UCLA eventually.

And he managed it in January 1964, after finally getting his parents' permission (though over 18 now, presumably he still needed a bit of financial assistance). Just before enrolling at UCLA, Jim visited his father (now a captain) on board his ship; though Jim had just had a haircut (to please his dad), it wasn't short *enough* , and his father made him have another one, this time a military cut from the ship's barber.

At the theatre arts department of UCLA, Jim majored in film technique. He also studied booze and philosophy and – when he could sneak off to visit whores in Mexico – sex. Though he returned to the parental home for holidays, he stayed as short a time as possible – and then simply stopped going at all. Not that he produced *that* much in the way of finished visual art... except for the obligatory end-of-year film. According to Morrison's fellow student Richard Blackburn, this featured "a girl doing a striptease on top of a television set tuned to a Nazi storm trooper rally, people rioting in a theatre when the stag film they're watching breaks down, a giant close-up of Jim taking a hit off a monstro-joint while he gave the audience the Big Wind!" Jim also worked as a cameraman on at least one other student film, called *Patient 411*, about a male prostitute who is given electro-shocks by behavioural scientists in a *Clockwork Orange* style-treatment. During this period he also wrote down his thoughts on film in an essay that would later be published as *The Lords: Notes On Vision*.

Jim graduated from UCLA in the summer of '65 (but only *just* – and it would appear this was basically an act of charity on the college's part), but didn't bother to attend the graduation ceremony. He'd already left, storming out a couple of days after the one and only screening of his end-of-year film had attracted extremely negative comments from both staff and students. But film would remain an abiding passion for Morrison, who later completed two features: *A Feast Of Friends* with two friends from UCLA, and *Hwy* ("about a hitch-hiker coming from Nature into the city"). He also made promotional films for 'Break On Through' and 'The Unknown Soldier', and shortly before his death had completed a screenplay for *The Adept*, which he had co-written with hip playwright Michael McClure.

Jim now severed all communication with his family, even burning cheques they sent him. Besides the fact that – in the middle of the Vietnam war – having a father commanding an aircraft carrier wasn't exactly good for one's image, some real personal enmity also seems to have been involved. In a 1969 interview he said: "The most loving parents and relatives commit murder with smiles on their faces. They force us to destroy the person we really are: a subtle kind of murder..." Your patient, Dr Freud. (According to Jerry Hopkins, after Jim became famous his mother managed to track him down by phone... but he refused to talk to her. And when she appeared in the front row of a Doors' concert, Jim sang the Oedipal section of 'The End' full into her face).

Meanwhile, Jim had also moved out of his apartment and was living wherever he could find a bed: mainly on friends' couches and floors. In large part, this probably all had to do with Jim's desire to vanish for a while. Having left college, he was now eligible for the draft. He moved to Venice Beach, living from June until August '65 with Dennis Jakob, and then on the roof of a warehouse. A friend later claimed that throughout these months Morrison ate LSD "like candy". Acid was still legal then, and sold over the counter in hip Venice boutiques. Jim had been smoking marijuana and boozing for years; it was inevitable he'd try acid, which was then being touted by Timothy Leary and Richard Alpert as being the answer to just about everything. Acid has a tendency to bring out hidden aspects of a person's personality (and not always for the good); with Jim it brought an unsuspected talent to the surface. Despite never having had any particular affinity for music (he'd had vague thoughts of becoming a writer or a sociologist), Jim "just started hearing songs." Then, as he later told *Rolling Stone*'s Jerry

Hopkins, he was overcome by a musical vision: "I heard in my head a whole concert situation, with a band and singing and an audience: a large audience. Those first five or six songs I wrote, I was just taking notes at a fantastic rock concert that was going on inside my head. And once I had written the songs, I just had to sing them."

It seems that acid was pretty much all that Morrison was living on that summer (and he continued taking it, in prodigious doses, throughout the next couple of years); his weight dropped from 160 lb to under 135 lb, and his cheekbones emerged from his puppy fat for the first time. And that August, in the beautiful hot summer of 1965, Jim Morrison bumped into someone he'd known at UCLA: Ray Manzarek.

Raymond Daniel Manzarek was born in Chicago on December 2, 1939 (or 1942, as his Elektra biography claims), and studied piano from the age of nine or ten. "I hated it for the first four years, until I learned how to do it – then suddenly it became fun. I first heard 'race music', as it was then called, when I was about twelve or thirteen, and from then on I was hooked. Listened to Al Benson, Big Bill Hill – they were disc jockeys in Chicago at the time – and my piano playing changed. I started to be influenced by jazz, learned how to play that stride piano with my left hand, and I knew that was it – stuff with a beat. Jazz, blues, rock..." Though Manzarek studied classical piano at the Chicago Conservatory, he was more interested in the blues clubs on Chicago's South Side. He completed a degree course in Economics at De Paul University before moving to UCLA to study law. Two weeks later he quit the course, and signed on for a management training course with the Western Bank of America. After about three months, Manzarek gave up on the possibilities of banking, and returned to UCLA to study cinematography.

Then, in December 1961, while reeling from a failed romance, Manzarek enlisted in the U.S. Army. By the time he realised that he'd made a hideous mistake, he was stationed in the Far East, playing in a Army band. In order to obtain an early discharge, Ray convinced an Army psychiatrist that he thought he was probably homosexual. He was duly discharged a year early, and returned to UCLA, where he resumed his film course and met Jim Morrison – who'd just arrived at the college – for the first time.

But – though a star pupil in the film school – Manzarek hadn't given up on music, and was still playing regularly in a band, Rick and The Ravens, alongside both his brothers, Rick and Jim: "We saw The Beatles and The Rolling Stones and thought – wait a minute, these guys are art students like us. Are you kiddin', these people are front-page news! People are going crazy over them! Girls are throwing themselves at them. They're making records; they're making money. We want this too!" The group recorded one single on Aura Records, which died (Ray was credited as 'Screaming Ray Daniels'!), and played every Friday and Saturday night at a club in Santa Monica called Turkey Joint West. As Manzarek recalls, it was here that Jim Morrison made his stage début: "I was in school and it was like a part-time job... I'd make about $35 a night, which was OK – it paid for the classes. That was the first time Jim ever sang on a stage. A whole bunch of guys from UCLA film school would come down, and there wasn't usually anyone in the club, so I'd call them all up on stage and we'd have about twenty guys, singing, jumping, screaming songs like 'Louie, Louie'."

When a band member quit on the eve of a Ravens' gig supporting Sonny & Cher, Manzarek found himself in dire need of an extra musician to make up the six-piece band stipulated in the contract, and for some reason thought of Jim Morrison. So Jim duly appeared on stage wearing an (unplugged) guitar, and just stood there with his back to the audience. Despite this low profile and (in real terms) non-existent contribution, Morrison later said the gig had "opened up a whole new world that I wasn't aware of – a free, exciting, strange, tense landscape."

Jim took his fee for the gig and split in the general direction of Venice Beach – where, months later, Manzarek ran into him again: "A beautiful California summer day, the middle of August, and who should come walking down the beach but Jim Morrison. I said, 'Hey man, I thought you were going to New York', and he said, 'Well, I was, but I decided to stay here. I've been at a friend's house, up on his rooftop, writing songs'."

They got talking about music and, as Manzarek sat in the sand, Morrison recited his lyrics for a song titled 'Moonlight Drive'. As Manzarek told it years later: "When he sang those lines, 'Let's swim to the moon/Let's climb through the tide/Penetrate the evening/That the city sleeps to hide', I said, that's it... It seemed as though, if we got a group together we could make a million dollars."

The new, slimmed, Jim even looked the part of a rock superstar (Manzarek thought he looked like Michelangelo's David), while the angular, studious Manzarek could provide the perfect counterbalance to Morrison's wild streak ("I can just look at Ray and know when I've gone too far," Morrison admitted years later). They decided to name their group The Doors, after Aldous Huxley's psychedelic memoir *The Doors of Perception* (though Huxley had himself been quoting William Blake: "If the doors of perception were cleansed, everything would appear to man as it truly is, infinite"). The name was a clear pointer to their own drug experimentation (and thus a shrewd commercial move, given the rise of the psychedelic culture), as Manzarek recalls: "At the time, we had been ingesting a lot of psychedelic chemicals, so the doors of perception were cleansed in our own minds, so we saw music as a vehicle to, in a sense, become a proselytiser of a new religion, a religion of self, of each man as God. That was the original idea behind The Doors, using music and Jim's brilliant lyrics." (Interestingly, Morrison had first come up with the name while at UCLA, suggesting to fellow-student Dennis Jakob that they form a duo called The Doors: Open and Closed).

Jim moved in with Manzarek, and they worked on Jim's songs for a couple of weeks before starting rehearsals with Ray's brothers Rick and Jim (on piano and guitar), using whatever drummers and bassists they could find. Then Manzarek, who was a devotee of Maharishi Mahesh Yogi, discovered John Densmore in the Maharishi's Los Angeles meditation centre. (Robbie Krieger was also into Transcendental Meditation, making three out of four of the final Doors devotees – how they managed to put up with a character as radically different in outlook from them as Morrison is a bigger mystery than any surrounding Jim's death.)

John Paul Densmore was born on December 1, 1944, in Santa Monica, and had been playing drums – particularly jazz drums – since the age of twelve. "I got my first set of drums when I was in Junior High. I played sort of symphonic music in High School – timpani, snare – then I played jazz for three years; sessions in Compton and Topanga Canyon." He played in a group called Terry Driscoll and The Twilighters (of whom nothing else is known) before joining The Psychedelic Rangers alongside guitarist Robert Krieger. (The Rangers recorded one song, 'Paranoia Blues', which remains unreleased to this day.) Then someone pointed Densmore out to Manzarek as being a drummer: "I went up to John and said, 'Listen man, I'm a keyboard player and I've got this great singer-songwriter and we're trying to get a band together. We need a drummer – would you be interested?' He said, 'Sure, why not?'"

John began rehearsing with the group, which still included Ray's brothers. Confronted with Jim's lyrics, Densmore thought: "Their songs were really far out

to me... I didn't understand very much; but then I figured, I'm the drummer, not the lyricist." Around this time, Morrison supposedly wrote to his parents, telling them he'd finished with college and was now in a rock band. Their response was reportedly angry, and Jim never wrote to them again.

For a while they had a female bass player (name unknown), who played on the demo tape the group recorded during three hours in September 1965 at World Pacific Studios (Aura Records owed Manzarek free studio time). Six songs were recorded: 'Moonlight Drive', 'Hello, I Love You', 'My Eyes Have Seen You', 'End Of The Night', 'Summer's Almost Gone' and 'Go Insane' (also known as 'A Little Game', and later to re-surface as a section of 'Celebration Of The Lizard').

Three acetates were made of the demo, and Manzarek, Morrison and Densmore touted them all over Los Angeles, trying to interest record companies. They met with zero success until Columbia executive Billy James (who had been instrumental in signing The Byrds)

decided to sign them up. With spectacular timing, Ray's brothers chose this moment to quit the group – and though they could live without a piano player, The Doors definitely needed a replacement guitarist.

Fortunately, there was an ideal candidate available. Robby Krieger had played with John Densmore in a group called The Psychedelic Rangers, and had also been present at the Maharishi's centre when Manzarek met Densmore. Then, Manzarek hadn't needed his services; now, he did, and called him with an invitation to rehearse.

Robert Alan Krieger was born on January 8, 1946, in Los Angeles, and was thus the youngest of the group. He'd also been raised with music, as he'd later recall: "There was a lot of classical music in my house – in fact, the first music I heard that I liked was 'Peter & The Wolf'. I think I was about seven. Then... I listened to rock'n'roll on the radio a lot: Fats Domino, Elvis Presley, The Platters. My father liked marching music, and I started playing trumpet at ten, but nothing came of that. So I began playing blues piano –

without lessons – then, at seventeen, I started playing guitar. Got my own when I was eighteen; it was a Mexican flamenco guitar, and I took flamenco lessons for a few months, until records got me into the blues, the newer rock'n'roll, like Paul Butterfield. If he hadn't gone electric, I probably wouldn't have got into rock'n'roll. I wanted to learn jazz, really. I got to know some people who did rock'n'roll with jazz, and I thought I would make money playing music."

Once they began rehearsals, it was obvious to Manzarek from the start that Krieger – who was studying psychology at UCLA – and his distinctive bottleneck guitar sound was exactly what The Doors needed to complete their concoction: "I said, 'This is it, this is the best musical experience I've ever had.' Of course, we were a little high at the time, but it was just... right, it was right from the beginning."

They rehearsed all week, and at weekends played any gig they could get: weddings, birthdays, whatever. Mainly they played crowd-pleasing standards like 'Louie, Louie' and 'Gloria', with Morrison still shyly standing with his back to the audience, and Ray doing most (if not all) of the singing. Nothing much was happening on the Columbia front – Billy James was trying to find a producer for them. But Columbia at least bought the group some equipment, including the Vox organ Manzarek played on The Doors' first three albums.

By December they were ready enough to audition for clubs, seeking a residency – but were consistently turned down by everybody, seemingly because of their lack of a bass player (they'd auditioned several, but hadn't found any kindred spirits). Then, by chance, Manzarek discovered the wonders of the Fender Rhodes piano bass, a keyboard which sounded like a bass guitar. Since playing boogie-woogie piano had taught Ray the rudiments of how to handle two sets of keyboards at once, he figured "the hell with a bass player."

And Morrison was slowly becoming more confident as they worked on their own material. Asked in 1981 by Jesse Nash whether the band's music had really been that much influenced by acid, Robby Krieger replied: "Uhm ... yeah. Especially songs written by Jim. He was taking a lot of LSD. I had taken LSD, but stopped before The Doors were formed. If I'd continued to take LSD, I thought I'd go crazy. And with Jim, the rest of the band had to be super straight in order to balance him off. If we were messed up, then who would take care of Jim? LSD did influence our music as far as the whole aura of universal subjects and more cerebral stuff like that."

Not that Morrison was intent on hogging the limelight, as Krieger recalls: "One day, Jim said: 'Everybody go home and write some songs, because we don't have enough songs'. I knew if I were to write a song for Jim it had to be pretty heavy, because Jim's songs were very heavy. So I knew it had to be about earth, air, fire or water. I tried so many combinations: 'Come on baby, breathe my air... come on baby, share my earth'. Shit like that, man. It was pretty embarrassing until I finally got

it to 'come on baby, light my fire'. That knocked Jim out."

Krieger also confirms that most of the first couple of albums' worth of songs had been written *very* early on: "Jim wrote most of his songs when he lived with this guy named Dennis Jakob, and Dennis had this great dope. When he would smoke this dope with Dennis... well, the songs would just pop into Jim's head and he'd write them the way they were on the final record without ever really having to change them. Pretty sensational, if you think about it. Most of Jim's songs made it to the album as first drafts! It's like the songs were already written and just waiting for someone to use them. It was weird."

In January 1966, The Doors got the break they were waiting for: they became the house band at the London Fog club on Sunset Strip. The fact that the owner's name was Jesse James should give you some idea of the club's clientèle: a mixture of drunks, sailors, hookers – and whatever acid heads and weirdos had drifted in on the evening breeze. Half the time, the joint was empty. They played seven nights a week, four sets a night, for five dollars each (ten at weekends), playing bar band blues and honing their own material (which at this time included 'Hello, I Love You', 'Light My Fire', 'Waiting For The Sun' and 'Break On Through'). By the time they got around to recording this material, they knew it so well that they were able to record pretty much live. As Ray tells it, "Because of all the time we had to fill on stage, we started extending songs, taking them into areas that we didn't know they would go into... and playing stoned every night. It was the great summer of acid, and we really got into a lot of improvisation, and I think that the fact that no one was at that club really helped us to develop what The Doors became."

In April, things started to go badly wrong: after four months at the Fog, they were fired. They bought their way out of the Columbia deal around the same time, but that was more a relief than anything else, as the label hadn't been overly enthusiastic (Ray : "A guy called Larry Marks came down to the Fog one night and said, 'I'm your producer' ... and we never saw him again"). More seriously, Morrison – who'd attempted to defer his draft eligibility by signing on for classes at UCLA, but had blown it by not actually showing up in the classroom – was classified A-1, and was told to report to his draft board in May. But almost immediately, they were signed up to be the house band at the more prestigious Whiskey-A-Go-Go club, at $135 each per week. And Jim got out of the draft easily enough, by altering his heartbeat with a handful of assorted drugs and claiming to be gay.

After an uneasy start, The Doors settled into their residency at the Whiskey, the hip hub of Sunset Strip, where seemingly half the people on the street were out of their brains on acid that summer. In San Francisco, they preached love and peace; in LA the counter culture had collided with Hollywood, and the general vibe was much brasher and noisier... just as The Doors were brasher than, say, Jefferson Airplane. Jim's hair had grown long, and was flowing over his shirt collar like a tide; he looked like Hamlet. Hamlet

on acid, that is. He was already wearing the trademark leather trousers, plus all manner of leather and lizard (he had a snakeskin suit) clothing, all made (and constantly repaired) by his friend January Jansen. When Jim hit the stage, he made a *big* impact.

Publicist Derek Taylor remembers seeing them there in early 1966, "doing strange things with sounds and words, Morrison playing with the microphone up against the speakers and singing some very finely aimed, original songs. They were a support act for Captain Beefheart at the Whiskey-A-Go-Go in Los Angeles; the place was not full." They played the Whiskey for a solid six months, as support to – amongst others – Love, The Turtles, The Byrds, Buffalo Springfield and Them. In addition to original material, they were also playing classic covers like 'In The Midnight Hour', 'Money', 'Little Red Rooster' and 'Hoochie Coochie Man'. When Them played the Whiskey, the two Morrisons (Van and Jim) improvised an extended jam... on 'Gloria', naturally. The

Doors *always* played loud, attempting to blow the headliners offstage, and quickly developed a steady following who'd turn up just to see what new stunt Jim would pull. Morrison would frequently turn up drunk or stoned (or both), indulging in acrobatics and a barrage of innuendo.

Morrison's self-confidence on stage had grown as he started to get chased by female fans, and he was obviously the group's star attraction. But he'd also been going steady since September '65 with a pretty 18-year-old California redhead, Pamela Courson, who'd just dropped out of art school. They had plenty in common (her father was in the naval reserve), and he enjoyed educating her in his artistic tastes (she referred to herself as "Jim's creation"). And there's no doubt that he returned her love – he often referred to her as his "cosmic mate" – and the couple remained together until Jim's death. But he was by no means ever faithful to her; he got propositioned a lot now, and often accepted.

One female acquaintance from 1966 had her own theories about Jim's promiscuity: "Fag. That's what I thought when I first saw him. Hated women. I think the acid revealed the homosexual inside him and it drove him crazy. I thought Jim was a total banana. He used to drop by my place and I was afraid to leave my small son around when he came in. The couple of times I left him alone, he opened up cans of tuna fish and smeared the stuff all over the walls." Not exactly the ideal house guest.

Right from the start, live performance for Morrison was an exploration of subversion and the theatre of confrontation. As he later explained it, "America was conceived in violence. Americans are attracted to violence. They attach themselves to processed violence, out of cans. They're TV-hypnotised – TV is the invisible protective shield against bare reality. Twentieth-century culture's disease is the inability to feel any reality. People cluster to TV, soap operas, movies, theatre, pop idols, and they have wild emotions over symbols. But in the reality of their own lives, they're emotionally dead."

All of this angst surfaced on stage one night when a tripping Jim decided to improvise for the first time the famous Freudian/Oedipal passage in the middle of 'The End'. Now, saying 'fuck' on stage in 1966 was pretty much unheard of; saying it in this context was undreamed of. The audience were shocked, the club's management apoplectic. As Lester Bangs later wrote of the song: "It was the first major statement of The Doors' perennial themes: dread, violence, guilt without possibility of redemption, miscarriages of love, and, most of all, death." It also got them fired from the Whiskey on the spot... but not before Arthur Lee of Love had taken Elektra boss Jac Holzman there to catch The Doors' act. Elektra at the time was a predominantly folkie label, looking for more rock acts like Love to sign. After seeing the band a couple of times, Holzman finally offered them a deal, which included (almost) complete artistic control. The Doors got themselves a lawyer (the splendidly named Max Fink), played hard-to-get just long enough, then signed the Elektra contract. Fortunately, the man chosen by Holzman to produce them – Paul A. Rothchild – had also managed to catch their act at the Whiskey just days before they got fired, and knew what fire they were capable of. All he had to do was provide the matches.

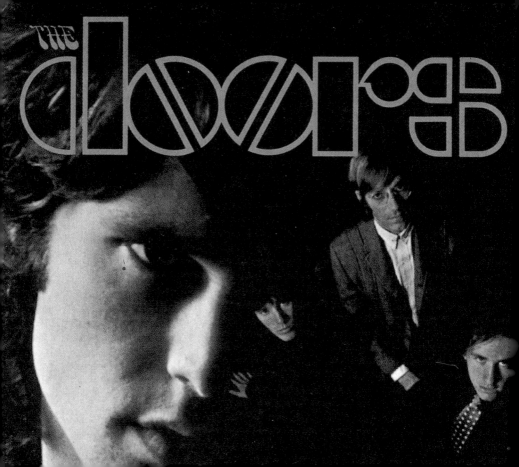

ORIGINAL ISSUE – ELEKTRA EKS 74007

The Doors began recording their first album in September 1966 at Sunset Sound Studio in Los Angeles, with Rothchild producing and Bruce Botnick as engineer. This team would work on (almost) all The Doors' recorded output in the years to come, and as Manzarek later recalled, the group's working relationship with Rothchild was... "a marriage made in heaven. Paul was just what we needed. He came down to the Whiskey a couple of nights and we found him to be a man of like mind, a man who knew his poetry, a man who knew his jazz, rock'n'roll and folk music and an excellent producer. He was very strong in the studio, and yet he knew when to give us our heads and when we needed to go in our own directions. He never really got in our way... he never really said, 'Well, don't do it that way, do it this way.' Any suggestion he'd have to offer would always be, 'Well, listen you guys, what do you think about doing it this way?' And many times his suggestions were correct and we'd say, 'Okay, that sounds like a good idea, Paul – let's do it that way.' Paul was an excellent manipulator in the studio."

As Rothchild tells it, he was content to give the group their head, going for atmosphere over technical perfection: "We didn't stop at a perfect take, we stopped at one we felt had the muse in it. That was the most important thing, for the take to have the feel, even if there were musical errors. When the muse came *that* was the take." At least two tracks were recorded that never made it to the finished album, one of which was 'Moonlight Drive', the song which had (kind of) started it all. Krieger: "Actually, that was the first song we recorded. Probably the reason it wasn't on the first album was because, as it was the first we did, it was probably the worst recorded. So, we re-recorded it for the second album... but I

still have the tape, the first tape, and it sounds pretty good."

Sunset was only a 4-track studio (the standard for the time), but this didn't prove any problem for The Doors, who knew their material so well that they were able to record most songs in two or three takes, dubbing the vocals afterwards. The whole album was recorded in two weeks (mixing took another five), but it wasn't all easy: one problem was that Ray's keyboard bass simply didn't sound good on tape (he abandoned its use in the studio after this). Some bass parts were over-dubbed, but most of the tracks were left untouched.

And there was one other major problem: Jim, who was still living rough, wandering the streets of West LA and sleeping wherever (and with whomever) he could. He was also taking huge quantities of various drugs: LSD, peyote, grass, amyl nitrate, mescaline… and alcohol, which would sadly become the overriding force in his life from now on. One take of 'The End' had to be abandoned because Jim was too out of it on a mixture of booze and acid that day. Though probably still tripping, he managed to get it right the following morning, as Rothchild recalls: "That half hour when we recorded 'The End' was one of the most beautiful moments I've ever had in a recording studio. I was totally overwhelmed. Normally, the producer sits there just listening for all the things that are right and anything about to go wrong, but for this take I was completely sucked up into it, absolutely audience. The studio was completely dark except for a candle in Jim's booth and the VU meters on the mixing board; all the other lights were off, it was a magic moment, and it was almost a shock when the song was over. It was like, yeah, *that's* the end, that's the statement – it can't go any further. There were about four other people in the control room, and we realised the tapes were still rolling, because Bruce, the engineer, was also completely sucked into it. His head was on the console and he was just absolutely immersed in the take – he became audience too… so the muse did visit the studio that time, and all of us were audience. The machines knew what to do, I guess…" For the album version (the first time they'd performed the song since it got them fired from the Whiskey) Morrison replaces the blatant "fuck you" with an inarticulate, animal moan – but the meaning was still clear.

When the album was finished, The Doors flew to New York where they played the hip Manhattan club Ondine's, and met with Elektra to discuss publishing, photo sessions, and promotion in general. They all took their music deadly seriously, and expected their company to present them that way – and that's how they come across in early interviews. As Krieger said at the time, "This group is so serious. It's the most serious group that ever was, that ever will be." Manzarek, meanwhile, attempted to explain their Huxley/Blake name-tag: "There are things you know about, and things you don't – the known and the unknown – and in between are the doors. That's us. We're saying that you're not only spirit, you're also this very sensuous being, and that's not evil. It's a really beautiful thing. Hell seems so much more fascinating and bizarre than heaven. You have to 'break on through to the other side' to become the whole being."

And appropriately enough, it was decided that the first single to be released from the album would be 'Break On Through' (though Elektra boss Jac Holzman insisted that the radio-sensitive controversial word "high" be edited out of the song for the single release). Both the single and album were released in January 1967.

The Doors' contains just two cover versions: Bertolt Brecht and Kurt Weill's 'Alabama Song (Whisky Bar)' from their 1929 opera *Aufstieg Und Fall Der Stadt Mahagonny* (which was included at Manzarek's suggestion; The Doors would also on occasion feature another Brecht & Weill song, 'Mack The Knife', from *The Threepenny Opera*, in live performance), and Willie Dixon's 'Back Door Man' (originally a hit for Howlin' Wolf). All the other songs were originals, with lyrics by Jim (except for 'Light My Fire', which was written by Krieger – though Jim made some lyrical suggestions) and music by all four Doors.

Its release caused quite an impact, though most reviewers inevitably concentrated on 'The End', which did seem to sum up the band's dark appeal ("The Stones were dirty but The Doors were *dread*," Lester Bangs observed in retrospect). And they *were* harsher, wilder and darker than anything else the Love Generation was producing; and, prior to Hendrix, Jim's obvious sexual appeal was more or less unique among the newer bands (very few – if any – 14-year-old girls had crushes on Country Joe). And the record company knew it, too; though the album's back cover photo gave equal space to all four Doors, on the front cover Jim's face dominates the montage, taking up over half the cover. A pattern was being established.

Strange Days

ORIGINAL ISSUE – ELEKTRA EKS 74014

In January 1967, as their début single and album hit the record stores, The Doors played their first gig in San Francisco, supporting Sopwith Camel and The Young Rascals at the Fillmore. Within weeks they were back in town, this time supporting Local Heroes and The Grateful Dead. They'd obviously done their usual trick of trying to blow the headliners off stage, and must have succeeded-for their third SF gig, at the Avalon Ballroom in March, The Doors were the headline act.

During these months they also played numerous gigs in LA, where 'Break On Through' made the Top Ten (though elsewhere it was almost totally ignored). Jim was by now living semi-permanently (i.e. whenever he remembered to go home) with Pam – and she had already acquired a taste for heroin, a taste she kept secret from Jim. In the last week of March, the group played another week-long residency at Ondine's in New York before returning to LA to record a 'single' version of 'Light My Fire'.

Based on audience reaction, the song was the obvious choice for a follow-up single. However, the album version was thought too long for radio airplay, and so the band agreed to record a new, shorter version. But the results were less than dynamic, so Paul Rothchild simply edited the album version, cutting a chunk out of the instrumental break. This abbreviated version of 'Light My Fire' was released as a single in April, and met with as little immediate impact as 'Break On Through'. But the single wasn't dead, merely sleeping; in early June it finally entered the national Top 100, reaching number one in the last week of July. Boosted by the amount of airplay the single was getting, the album rose up the charts to number two (and would almost certainly have made number one if 'Sergeant Pepper's Lonely Hearts Club Band' hadn't blocked it), remaining on the album charts for the next two years.

'Light My Fire' was subsequently covered by Jose Feliciano, among hundreds of others (including the Ecclesfield School Choir, Ted Heath and Jonathan King), improbably establishing itself as a standard. As Krieger said in 1981: "To be honest, I don't care if people think that Jim wrote all the songs, but if they think Jose Feliciano wrote them, that really gets me pissed off." What pissed Jim Morrison off, some years later, was learning that the other Doors had considered letting Buick use the song to advertise their cars. Worse, they hadn't even consulted him about it (he was in London at the time). Though he headed off the attempt (by putting pressure on Jac Holzman not to allow the sale), he was mightily peeved with his fellow band members. "I don't have partners anymore – I have associates," he is reputed to have told one friend. And one story has it that Morrison was so miffed by news of the Buick deal that he deliberately rammed sixteen Buicks parked on the Strip before writing off his own Porsche into a fence. Since Morrison didn't even have a driver's licence at the time, perhaps we can write the story off as apocryphal. Then again, that wouldn't have stopped him, so perhaps not.

Meanwhile, back in 1967, The Doors decided they needed a manager. Not that their affairs were particularly complicated – they simply split *everything* (including song publishing) four ways. But success brought fandemonium to be fended and business offers to be sifted through; they needed someone to get them a proper booking agency and a publicist, *and* to keep a watchful eye on the increasingly maverick Morrison. After looking at various management companies, they signed a deal (the standard 15%, plus expenses) with Asher Down and his partner Sal Bonafede. Their new managers quickly got the group signed with a booking agent and a publicist, and their concert fee increased dramatically overnight.

They headlined at the Fillmore West in June, then flew to New York, where they played one night at the Village Theater, followed by a three-week residency at the Scene Club. The club shut down during the three-day-long Monterey Pop Festival, the bill for which included virtually every major West Coast band *but* The Doors (according to Festival director John Simon, the group had been overlooked until it was just too late to add them to the bill). Jim was evidently miffed at not being included, drinking heavily, and being generally sullen. But then the album was released, to general acclaim, and things began to look brighter. Jim had a brief fling with chanteuse Nico, but returned to Pamela the next day.

Given their chart success, the group were in optimistic mood when they returned to Sunset Sound in August to record the next album. Once again Rothchild and Botnick were at the controls but, in the months since the band had completed their début, the studio had upgraded its mixing deck.

As Manzarek later recalled: "'Strange Days' is when we began to experiment with the studio itself, as an instrument to be played. It was now 8-track and we thought, 'My goodness, how amazing! We can do all kinds of things – we can do overdubs, we can do this, we can do that... we've got eight tracks to play with!' It seems like nothing today, in these times of thirty-two or even forty-eight track recording, but those eight tracks to us were really liberating. So, at that point, we began to play... it became five people: keyboards, drums, guitar, vocalist and studio."

The album would include one highly experimental track – a version of a poem Jim wrote while still in high school called 'Horse Latitudes'. Botnick and Rothchild created a backing track of white noise, over which the other Doors plucked instruments randomly (and beat coconut shells, and dropped Coke bottles into metal bins), while – over the top of all this – Morrison recited his highly unusual poem: "It's about the Doldrums where sailing ships from Spain would get stuck. In order to lighten the vessel, they had to throw things overboard; their major cargo was working horses for the New World, and this song is about that moment when the horse is in the air. I imagine it must have been hard to get them over the side, 'cause when they got to the edge, they probably started chucking and kicking... and it must have been hell for the men to watch, too, because horses can swim for a while, but then they lose their strength and just go down... slowly sink away."

There was psychedelic strangeness throughout, from the echoing tones on the title track (which was one of the first uses of the Moog synthesiser – The Doors were beaten to the punch only by The Beach Boys and The Monkees), to the backwards cymbal on 'I Can't See Your Face In My Mind'. As with their début, they closed the album with the longest track. This time it was 'When The Music's Over', the lyrics of which featured what was to become a rallying cry for the new Left (and for the young in general): "We want the world and we want it now." If it lacked the searing impact of their first album, that was only to be expected – this time, people had more of an idea what to expect – but it's still a first-rate album.

Recording sessions were still going on when 'People Are Strange' was released as a single in September 1967, as a taster of the album to come. It reached number twelve on the charts.

Morrison had hated the cover of the first album, and wanted something better – he suggested a shot of the band surrounded by thirty dogs "but we couldn't get the dogs. Everyone was saying, 'What are the dogs for?' And I said that it was symbolic – that it spelled God backwards." Doubtless fearful of accusations of Satanism, Elektra rejected the idea and "finally we ended up leaving it to the art director and the photographer", who came up with the idea of using circus side-show freaks for the cover photograph (it was later used by underground magazine *Oz* as a front cover). Morrison himself approved of the finished shot by photographer Joel Brodsky: "It looked European. It was better than having our fucking faces on it, anyway."

'Strange Days' was released in October 1967. This time, all the songs were Doors' originals (Krieger wrote the lyrics to 'You're Lost Little Girl' and 'Love Me Two Times', while Jim wrote the rest; the music was once again by all four Doors). Many of the songs had been around for quite a while, but are still radically different from the work of most of their contemporaries: in the brightness of the Summer of Love, The Doors still embraced dark weirdness.

And it was popular, too – if Jim Morrison truly wanted the world, and wanted it now, for a while it looked like he might even get it. Within two months of its release 'Strange Days' rose to number three on the album charts, and stayed on the charts for over a year. For most of this period, the group were almost constantly touring.

And in live performance, Jim was constantly pushing the boundaries, climbing up stage curtains or walking tightrope-style down the front of the stage before pitching headlong into the crowd. He'd signal for silence in the middle of a song – and stay silent until the audience's restlessness grew unbearable (he kept it up for four minutes on one occasion), at which point he'd signal the band to resume the song once more.

"It was total theatre," was Densmore's description of Jim's live antics. "It wasn't planned or conceived in the studio. It was fairly subconscious. Jim was magical – he never quite knew what he was going to do each night, and that's what was so exciting – the suspence, because obviously we didn't really know either. Our framework was our music, but it didn't seem that rigid; somehow we could go off on a tangent for twenty minutes or so, and Jim would stretch out, improvise some poetry and we'd vamp along – comment on his poetry and improvise for a while, then we'd get back into the chorus of the song... so that was what made it so exciting. Plus, he had a great rapport with the audience – he could really work 'em up!"

Straight after the concert where Jim had yelled "Fuck you!" straight into his mother's face, The Doors flew to New

York, to appear on the Ed Sullivan Show. Sullivan was enormously influential, and appearing on his show had helped both Elvis Presley and The Beatles break through to the huge viewing audience. The Doors were to perform 'Light My Fire', but there was just one problem: the CBS censor objected to the use of the word "higher" in the song's lyric. A substitute line was suggested, to which the group agreed but... Jim was Jim, and there was no way he'd go along with this straight media bullshit. During the live broadcast he sang the song – and the word – unaltered. He was told The Doors would never perform on the Sullivan show again, and he wasn't the least bit bothered.

In November, 'Love Me Two Times' was released as the next single (it reached number twenty-five). That was the good news; the bad news was that Jim's drinking was really getting out of hand. At a gig at San Francisco's Winterland, Morrison was drunk as a skunk, and the show stank like skunk stink.

The group's managers were concerned, but thought perhaps Jim was just

celebrating. '67 had been a good year for The Doors: two top five albums, three top thirty singles. The media were comparing Jim not only to James Dean, Marlon Brando and Bob Dylan, but also to Dionysius and Adonis.

But the year was to end badly. On December 9, 1967, the day after Jim's 24th birthday, The Doors played the New Haven Arena, in New Haven, Connecticut. Morrison was hanging around backstage, talking to a girl admirer in his dressing room; when that became overcrowded, they retired to the privacy of a shower stall. A policeman from the New Haven force discovered them there, and told them to move on. Jim, being Jim, told the cop to fuck off. Heated words were exchanged – and then the cop pulled out a can of Mace and sprayed Jim full in the face with it.

News of the incident was relayed to Ray Manzarek and Bill Siddons (the group's equipment manager, soon to become their personal manager), who ran to convince police that the person they were arresting (Jim was about to be driven to jail) was the lead singer of the group appearing there that night. Not wishing to provoke a crowd scene (the auditorium was already filled with thousands of expectant fans), the police chief apologised, Jim was released, and Manzarek and Siddons helped him get cleaned up. And that was that, or so everybody thought – incident over.

Not for Jim, it wasn't. He went on stage, eyes still bloodshot from the Mace, and did the show. And it was a good show, the audience was responsive and enthusiastic. Then, in the middle of the last number, 'Back Door Man', Morrison launched into a spontaneous rap, telling the audience about the incident backstage, how he'd been attacked for no good reason. And, as Bill Siddons later recalled: "He so humiliated the rationale of the police that he could have taken those thousands of kids and rallied them and they all would have died for him. It was unbelievable."

Police started to appear on stage at the end of the song, and the house lights went up. "Do you want to hear one more?"

Morrison asked the crowd, who bayed a giant 'Yes' in reply. "Then turn off the lights," Morrison said, in the general direction of the lighting booth, "turn off the fucking lights." This last comment was the final straw for the cop in charge. Lieutenant Kelly strode on stage, told Morrison he was under arrest, and told the crowd that the show was over. In the ensuing mêlée, two reporters and a photographer were also arrested, thus guaranteeing Jim maximum publicity.

Morrison was supposedly beaten up by two cops en route to the police station, where he was charged with a breach of the peace, giving an indecent and immoral exhibition, and resisting arrest. Bill Siddons paid the $1500 bail from the concert receipts, and they left town immediately. But this was only the *beginning* of Jim Morrison's troubles with the police, and over the next couple of years he must have wondered if they had 'Wanted' posters out for him.

On a happier note, just before Christmas, Ray Manzarek got married. Jim was best man.

Waiting for the sun

ORIGINAL ISSUE – ELEKTRA EKS 74014

In early January 1968, The Doors returned to Sunset Sound, to record their third album. And the trouble with third albums, as Robbie Krieger explains, is the 'third-album syndrome': "Usually, a group will have enough songs in their repertoire to record one, or maybe two albums, and then what'll happen is they go on tour and they don't have any time to write any more stuff. So, by the third album you find yourself trying to write stuff in the studio, and it shows, usually."

Initially, a lack of material didn't seem that big a problem, as one whole side of the album was to be taken up by Morrison's epic song-poem 'The Celebration Of The Lizard'. As with 'The End', this song had evolved over a long period of time, and had seven distinct sections. But in the studio, it just didn't work, and only Morrison was happy with the (25-minute-long) version they actually recorded; in the end, Rothchild and the other Doors overruled him, and it was duly dumped... though one section – 'Not To Touch The Earth', which had something resembling a tune – did see inclusion on the finished album. To compound the confusion, the complete 'Celebration Of The Lizard' lyrics were reproduced on the album's gatefold sleeve (described as "lyrics to a theatre composition by The Doors"). Reptile rock had seemingly gotten more pretentious (not to mention egomaniacal) in the decade since 'See You Later Alligator', with Morrison proclaiming : "I am the Lizard King/I can do anything". The 'Lizard King' tag was a gift to the media, who mined it for all it was worth, aided by some of Jim's own musings: "The lizard and the snake are equated with the subconscious forces of evil... Even if you've never seen one, a snake seems to embody everything that we fear. It ('Celebration Of The Lizard') is a kind of invitation to dark, evil forces." Jim later attempted (unsuccessfully) to shrug off the label: "It's all done tongue in cheek – I don't think people realise that it's not meant to be taken seriously. When you play the bad guy in a Western, that's not you – that's just something you keep for the show. I don't really take it seriously... that's supposed to be ironic." A theatrical presentation of 'Celebration' was mooted, but also came to nothing, and most people didn't get to hear the work in its entirety until a version was included on the 1970 live album, 'Absolutely Live'.

But the loss of 'Lizard' left them with a serious hole to fill, and little time to do it in. And for the first time the group had to learn how to work with a guest musician; Manzarek's keyboard bass hadn't really worked in the studio, so they'd decided to bring in a bassist (a practice that would become customary in the studio from now on) – Doug Lubahn, from Elektra band The Clear Light.

Jim's condition didn't help, either; he was by now outrageously drunk a large portion of the time. He'd taken to passing out in public (on one occasion at an airport Bill Siddons quietly shoved him under a bench, and covered the spectacle with his suitcases). He was violent and abusive; and it didn't help his performance any, either (if you want to hear Morrison at his musical worst – and you probably don't – there's a bootleg of Jimi Hendrix jamming at New York's Scene Club with sundry musical luminaries... including Jim, whose recorded burbling is so embarrassing that you wonder how he didn't just get booted offstage).

He was usually drunk when he arrived at the studio, often with a crowd of sycophantic hangers-on and groupies in tow. Unsurprisingly, the studio atmosphere wasn't exactly conducive to creativity. In fact, it got so bad that one night things reached boiling point for John Densmore, who threw his drumsticks across the studio and announced that he was quitting the band: "It was the third album syndrome... I was just frustrated. On a couple of nights, I felt… I was just hinting that I was dissatisfied, wanting to drop out, whatever. Maybe I was trying to say to Jim, don't be so self-destructive… " Densmore was persuaded to stay, but things were definitely *not* going well.

As if life wasn't stressful enough, The Doors chose this moment to split from their managers, borrowing the money from Elektra to buy back their management contract from Dann and Bonafede. This move was dictated not so much by business acumen as by the need for solidarity, as the Dann/Bonafede axis had been trying to persuade Jim to quit the group and go solo… and were also fuelling his booze problem with free whiskey. As a replacement, Robby Krieger asked their equipment manager, a 19-year-old surfer named Bill Siddons, if he'd consider becoming the new manager of The Doors. "What does a manager do?" Siddons wanted to know. "Well, just answer the phones and we'll have meetings and decide what to do," Krieger told him.

"It was absolutely stupid to hire me," Siddons said years later. "I had no idea what I was doing. They, on the other hand, were controlling their own destiny. They had discovered early in their career that a lot of people had a very different set of motives than theirs."

By March the group had managed to finish two tracks, 'The Unknown Soldier' and 'We Could Be So Good Together', which were released as a taster of the album to follow. 'Unknown Soldier' had evolved in concert in the same way as 'The End' had done, and was a favourite with concert audiences for its theatricality (evident just from hearing the studio version of the song); it was also overtly political, and its obvious anti-Vietnam War connotations ensured that it was big on the underground circuit – but its stance also effectively ruled out any chance of radio airplay, and it consequently only just made it into the Top Forty.

Meanwhile, the group were desperately trying to scrape together enough material to finish the album. There were a few early songs they hadn't recorded to date; most of the rest were written in the studio (and it shows), requiring constant re-takes since the group were so unfamiliar with them – something Morrison hated doing with a passion. Surprisingly, 'Waiting For The Sun' didn't make it to the album that bears its name (though it was better than many of the songs that did); and it's a remarkably patchy collection, though it has its moments. Apart from the two tracks released earlier and the extract from 'Lizard', the album's standout tracks must be 'Spanish Caravan', an impressive adaptation of a traditional flamenco piece, and the a capella medicine-man stomp of 'My Wild Love'.

There was also the anthemic 'Five To One', which carried another handy youth slogan: "the old get old and the young get younger/may take a week and it may take longer/they got the guns, but we got the numbers/gonna win, yeah we're taking over". Nobody could figure this one out for sure: 5 to 1 was said to be the ratio of whites to blacks in the USA, or the ratio of straight people to dope-smokers in LA, or... who knew? Most people took it to indicate a faith in the rising power

(and number) of youth; if so, Jim was sadly naïve – the establishment had both guns *and* numbers, as it turned out, and that autumn 10,000 Yippies got battered and maced into the ground by Chicago police at the Democratic Convention. But Morrison was only voicing the spirit of the times, the spirit of a generation which "blithely mistook its demographic proliferation for real political power", to quote from Lee & Shlain's excellent study of the era, *Acid Dreams* (Grove/Weidenfeld).

As if to underscore the ironies of The Doors' own position in the rock world (caught between the teenyboppers and the underground), the album also contained the group's poppiest (it's almost bubblegum) song to date, 'Hello I Love You'. Based around a riff that sounds suspiciously like The Kinks' 'All Day And All Of The Night', this one couldn't fail – as a single, it went to Number One on the U.S. charts, as did the album when it was released in July. Jim celebrated this success by announcing that he wanted to leave the group because this whole thing wasn't what he had expected or wanted;

Manzarek talked him into staying on, to see what the next six months might bring. Jim agreed, but he wasn't happy.

At a Chicago gig on May 10, he apparently decided to see how far he could take this rock star game, how far he could push an audience. He gave the performance of his life, whipping the audience into a frenzy. When the group didn't return for a third encore, the audience rioted and rushed the stage. Three months later, fans rushed the stage *during* a concert at New York's Singer Bowl, fought with police and threw wooden chairs at them. The concert had to be abandoned, but not before Pete Townshend of the Who (who were on the same bill) witnessed a young girl in the audience bleeding profusely and calling to Jim, who completely ignored her (or perhaps just didn't see her); Townshend used the incident as the basis for his song 'Sally Simpson' in 'Tommy'.

Jim was increasingly interested once again in other areas: in film, having worked on a promotional film (an almost revolutionary concept at the time) for the 'Unknown Soldier' single. (Given the song's subject matter, it received even less airplay on TV than on radio.) He was also working on a proposed Doors documentary, *Feast Of Friends*, with two old friends from UCLA, cameraman Paul Ferrara and editor Frank Lisciandro. And, encouraged by the response to the 'Lizard' lyrics, Jim began to explore the possibilities of getting his poetry published in book form.

At the beginning of September, The Doors embarked on their first European tour (of Britain, Denmark, West Germany and Holland), which kicked off with four London gigs (co-headlining with Jefferson Airplane) at the Roundhouse, on September 6 and 7 (two sets each night; tickets cost between 25/- and £2). Fanticipation ran high, as the 10,000 seats for the four concerts quickly sold out; Jefferson Airplane previewed their set with a free concert in Parliament Hill Fields, thus sparking rumours of a similar free Doors show (no such luck). Those who couldn't get tickets for the Roundhouse gigs were slightly consoled by the news that The Doors' set was to be filmed by Granada Television.

As the film's director John Sheppard later recalled: "The first night there was a massive conflict, there were a lot of egos clashing backstage because no one had worked out who was going to play first: The Doors or the Airplane. And the Airplane won. So the Friday night was just bad vibes: The Doors were in a bad mood because they lost out in the ego battle, although we preferred them to go first – it meant Granada paid less overtime. We were only shooting their first set anyway and whether the second night might have been better was simply not a question that was asked.

"Morrison was in a thoroughly pissed-off mood. The rest of the band were staying at the Royal Lancaster; he and his girlfriend had their own flat in Eaton Square, and he had already missed the sound check. And for one number he insisted on complete blackness – so there we are, filming the concert, and we have three minutes of blackness. And to cap it all, round about midnight the chief engineer came to me after we'd finished and said that we had a fault on video and that the whole of Friday night was lost anyway. So we now had to get everything on the Saturday. When we arrived at the Roundhouse it was all sweetness and light. Maybe someone had a word with Morrison, I don't know. Anyway, come the Saturday evening I was ready to do it right, the crew were up to the mark and The Doors played a fantastic set."

Underground DJ John Peel, who compèred the Roundhouse gigs, said that Britain had embraced The Doors the way America had once embraced The Beatles. He also later recalled a backstage interchange between Morrison and Elektra executive Clive Selwood: "Clive said to Morrison, 'Hey, we've got you a really groovy driver to drive you around'. And Morrison said, 'Listen, I don't want a really groovy driver, I just want a bloke who can drive'. And I thought that seemed to be a jolly useful maxim for a lot of things in life. God save me from the groovy driver, just give me somebody who can drive. I don't know if he ever said anything else wise, but that certainly was."

Granada's film, *The Doors Are Open*, shown the following month on British TV, suffered from weedy sound and bad lighting. The live footage was also irritatingly intercut with news film of the infamous Grosvenor Square anti-Vietnam War demonstration when mounted police attacked the demonstrators (Mick Jagger, hovering on the fringes of the demo, had been inspired to write 'Street Fighting Man'). Editing the footage in this manner (as pioneered by one-time music critic Tony Palmer... though Morrison's own films are similarly guilty) supposedly helped demonstrate rock's relevance and insight to the post-thirty intelligentsia; to anyone under thirty, it was just a pain. But Morrison – who later described their final London show as "one of the best we've ever done" – was highly pleased with the Granada film: "I thought the film was very exciting. To be on television, I think that's incredible. The thing is, the guys who made the film had a thesis of what it was going to be before we even came over. We were going to be the political rock group, and it also gave them the chance to whip out some of their anti-American sentiments, which they thought we were going to portray, and so they had their whole film before we came over... but I still think they made an exciting film."

Which is more than can be said for *Feast Of Friends*. After ploughing over $30,000 into the project, The Doors eventually decided that enough was enough, and filming was halted. Frank Lisciandro edited the film (with suggestions from Jim) – a mixture of live footage (including the Singer Bowl concert/riot) and backstage shots. But instead of using live sound for the concert scenes, studio versions of the songs were used instead; the result was a curiously unsuccessful mix of cinéma vérité (for which, read 'home movie') and pop video, though Morrison was still impressed (even if no one else was): "The first time I saw that film, I was pretty much taken aback, 'cause being on stage, being one of the central figures, I could only see it from my viewpoint. But then to see things as they really were... I suddenly realised that I was, to a degree, just a puppet, controlled by a lot of forces I understood only vaguely." These were ominous words: those forces would soon go out of Morrison's control entirely.

While in London, Jim met with American poet playwright Michael McClure, to discuss starring in a film of McClure's play *The Beard* as Billy the Kid, and the possibility of writing a screenplay together. According to McClure, they "made a poets' tour of the city through the strip joints of Soho to the Tate Museum (sic), and then took a moonlight ride with poet Christopher Logue to see the hospital which now stands on the site where Blake lived. We became brief habitués of the music clubs The Bag O'Nails and Arethusa's, where we saw Christine Keeler, movie stars, and drank glasses of Courvoisier and had philosophical talks with film directors." (I apparently missed meeting him in Portobello Road by about ten minutes; so it goes.). McClure

complimented Jim on his work and advised him to publish his poetry privately – which he subsequently did.

The rest of the European tour also went well... until they got to Amsterdam, where Morrison - who had swallowed two large lumps of hashish given to him earlier by fans, and (who had needless to say) also been drinking all day - ran on stage while Jefferson Airplane were playing, dancing enthusiastically. Then he collapsed. He was removed to hospital in a portable oxygen tent, while the band travelled on to the next town, where they performed as a trio without Jim. Back at the hospital, the doctor apparently told Bill and Cheri Simmons that , "this guy's liver is really not good. If he doesn't stop the drinking, he's not going to live." Despite this major signpost to his eventual fate, it's both sad and surprising that nobody around him seemed able to drag Jim Morrison back from the edge he was evidently hell-bent on toppling over.

Back in the States, Jim got himself a literary agent. He was enthusiastic about England, less so about Europe: "London was the best, I'd say. They really liked it. The rest was neither here nor there: limited enthusiasm. I got the idea they didn't like or dislike it... they didn't know how to express what they felt about it. But they really take music seriously over in Europe. It's not just the province of kids – they discuss it."

And The Doors continued to tour. The first couple of gigs went quietly, but concerts in St Louis, Cleveland, Phoenix and Chicago all hovered on the brink of chaos and rioting, occasionally plunging over the edge. It was as if the music was no longer enough; the audiences now demanded more – an event, a ritual, a rite or a riot. And the police were *always* there now, expecting (or perhaps even courting) trouble. Jim tried to write it all off as "just fun. We have fun, the cops have fun, the kids have fun. It's kind of a weird triangle." Krieger was a little less glib: "It always bothered me to have police hanging around the concerts, waiting to bust us on any word or thing that we did... but we expected it. It was all part of the trip. There were two forces working – one force of change, and the other force that wants

things to stay the same and not be too far out, and there's always the balance that has to be present there at those situations." But, as Morrison pointed out, if the cops weren't there, there'd be no authority to confront, and possibly no riot.

In December, The Doors went back to the studio, to begin sessions for the next album. And on December 8, Jim's 25th birthday, Cheri Simmons shared a poignant moment with him: "We were walking down the stairs of The Doors' office and he said to me, 'Well, I made it to 25, do you think I'll make it to 30?' And we both knew he wouldn't make it to 30."

the doors/the soft parade

the Soft Parade

ORIGINAL ISSUE – ELEKTRA EKS 75005

On Friday December 13, 1968, The Doors were headlining a concert at the Los Angeles Forum. Support acts were Jerry Lee Lewis and a Chinese folk musician, both of whom got heckled by a crowd impatient to see The Doors. When an over-enthusiastic fan threw lighted sparklers on stage, Jim lost patience with the baying crowd. "What are you doing here?" he asked them. "Why did you come tonight?" No response. "Well, we can play music all night, if that's what you want," Jim told them. "But that's not what you want, is it? You want something more, something different, something you ain't never seen before, don't you?" He paused. "Well, fuck you! We came to play music!" The group launched into a 40-minute version of 'Celebration Of The Lizard', with absolutely no stage theatrics from Jim – he just stood there, gripping the mike stand. The audience was stunned into silence.

But playing music was getting harder, as Morrison himself admitted: "When we had to carry our own equipment everywhere, we had no time to be creative; now we can focus our energies more intensively... the trouble is, we really don't see each other that much anymore. We're big time, so we go on tours, record, and in our free time, everyone splits off into their own scenes. When we record, we have to get all our ideas then. We can't build them night after night like we used to in the clubs. In the studio, creation isn't so natural."

It didn't sound like it either – as the December release of The Doors' new single 'Touch Me' (a taster from the album they were currently recording) – proved. Morrison seems ill at ease throughout the song (and, indeed the album), which featured a heavy use of a string section. The song was one of Krieger's, and with this album Morrison insisted for the first time that the songs' writers be individually credited, so as to distance himself from Krieger's lyrical output. Perhaps Jim was keeping his own creative juices back for his poetry, as he contributed surprisingly few songs to the album. Whatever, 'Touch Me' sounded almost like self-parody (live, Jim was known to substitute the words "suck me" for the title refrain; he'd refused to sing Krieger's original lyric, which was "hit me"); it's anodyne, anti-septic despite the risqué refrain, and seemingly cynically designed to appeal to the group's teenybopper female following. It still managed to get to number three on the charts, where it stayed for a couple of months.

Hit singles were probably the last thing Morrison wanted. He wanted to be taken seriously as a writer, and wanted The Doors to make a mark on their peer audience, not on teenyboppers. He hated his position as teenage idol, despised his role as sexy pin-up. It's probable that his gaining weight over the next few years was (at least in part) a deliberate attempt to dis-

tance himself from that image – as was growing a beard and dressing as shabbily as possible. And becoming a drunken slob? Partly, that may have been deliberate – Jim definitely wasn't above acting appallingly just to psych people out (or drive them away); then again, in his final years he also had a lot of other problems on his plate.

"I went through a period when I drank a lot," he admitted later that year. "I had a lot of pressure hanging over me that I couldn't handle, and I was also drinking as a way to cope with living in a crowded environment, and also as the product of boredom. But I enjoy drinking: it loosens people up and stimulates conversation sometimes. Somehow it's like gambling – you go out for a night of drinking, and you don't know where you'll end up the next morning. It could be good, could be a disaster. It's a throw of the dice." But he was still confident – almost certainly *overconfident* – that he had the problem under control. "I can gauge everything so's I can stay in one place; every sip is another chance at bliss."

At least he had a sense of humour. In January 1969, at Madison Square Garden, Morrison addressed half the adoring audience: "You are life," he proclaimed. Turning to the other side of the auditorium he announced, "You are death." Then, to the entire crowd, he said, "I straddle the fence, and my balls hurt." The fact that he was suffering from gonorrhoea at the time gives his remarks an added poignancy.

But live performance seemed to give him something special (and sorely lacking from his current experience in the studio) – the thrill of manipulating a crowd. "I was less theatrical, less artificial when I began," he admitted. "But now, the audiences we play for are much larger, the rooms much bigger. It's necessary to project more, to exaggerate, almost to the point of grotesqueness. I think that when you're a small dot at the end of a large arena, you have to make up for that lack of intimacy with expanded movements." The faults of stadium rock would become only too apparent with the advent of giant video screens that allowed the audience

(and the bands) a half-decent chance of seeing the stage action; the result was simply that many bands ended up parodying themselves.

Morrison definitely believed in the idea of rock concert as ritual ("a game is a closed field, a ring of death with sex at the centre, and performing is the only game I've got") and was optimistically confident about his chosen role as shaman ("Kids are the future. Kids you can change and mould and influence. That's what's important about a young audience – they're like clean paper waiting to be written on... and I'm the ink"). The result was that nobody knew what was going to happen at a Doors concert. Including The Doors. As Robbie recalled in 1972, "He used to listen, stop and listen to what the audience had to say. We didn't know what the hell was going on." Later that year Morrison commented on the joy he felt on stage: "The only time I really open up is on stage. I feel spiritual up there. Performing gives me a mask, a place to hide myself where I can reveal myself. I see it as more than performing, going on, doing songs, and leaving. I take everything personally, and don't really feel I've done a complete job unless we've gotten everybody in the theatre on common ground." On another occasion, he put it more simply: "I just try to give the kids a good time."

In February a second single 'Wishful Sinful' was released from the forthcoming album; it was similarly lacklustre. But something more dramatic (quite literally) happened that month: Jim finally got to see experimental performance troupe the Living Theater when they came to play the University of Southern California. The previous year, he'd read an article about them which read: "They are not really performers but a roving band of Paradise seekers, who define Paradise as total liberation, practising hypnology and advocating Paradise Now. Their presence and function are in direct opposition to that repressive totalitarian state known as law and order." Theirs was a theatre of confrontation, about breaking down the barriers between performer and audience, and it was right up Jim's alley; he went to every performance, and talked to as

many of the company as he could manage. On the final night he was there when the cast removed most of their clothing, and the police closed the show down. Jim was impressed

So, what happened when The Doors played the Dinner Key auditorium in Miami the very next night, March 1, may well have occurred because Morrison had been inspired by the Living Theater's performance and wanted to try some new tricks on a rock audience; then again, it may just have happened because he was drooling drunk and in a foul mood – he'd missed two flights in his journey from LA to Miami, and had (inevitably) passed the time boozing.

The concert kicked off an hour late, and Jim didn't bother with even *attempting* to sing: he wanted to talk to – or with – the audience instead. The band made several attempts to get him to sing, launching into songs in the hope that he'd tag along; he'd sing a couple of lines, then signal them to quit playing so he could get back to his rap. When they played the opening of 'Touch Me', it was the final straw. As

Manzarek told it later, "Jim said to the audience, 'That's enough. You didn't come here to hear music... you didn't show you my cock? Isn't that what you want?' So he took his shirt off and put it in front of himself, and started dancing

come here to see a good rock and roll band – you came here for something you've never seen before, something greater and bigger than you've ever experienced... What can I do? How 'bout if I around, holding his shirt down, covering his groin, and he pulled his shirt away – 'Did ya see it, did ya see it, there it is, look , I did it, I did it." If Morrison did actually flash anything that night, it's far more probable that

$80,000 on it – we were making our 'Sgt. Pepper'. Just to show how ridiculous things got, we imported Jesse McReynolds and Jimmy Buchanan, a fiddler and a picker, from North Carolina, to play one solo on one song." Though even Densmore admits the finished product is less than their greatest hour: "I enjoyed it for what it was," he says simply.

In 1970, Morrison had this to say about the album : "It kinda got out of control, and took too long in the making. It spread over nine months. An album should be like a book of stories strung together, some kind of unified feeling and style about it, and that's what 'The Soft Parade' lacks."

Morrison's lack of involvement in the album is strange considering that he believed – as he told one interviewer around this time – that albums had "replaced books... and movies. A movie you might see once, maybe twice, then later on television. But an album, it's more influential than any art form going. Everybody digs them, and some you listen to about fifty times. You measure your progress mentally by your records." And progression was what he knew the band needed; their commercial success was only incidental, and he was increasingly dismissive of the industry's obsession with having hit singles: "more and more, I think that the three-minute single is pointless."

He talked to the press a *lot*, opening up at length to Jerry Hopkins for *Rolling Stone* (and Jim was delighted when one of his poems was included in Hopkins' piece, credited to James Douglas Morrison, poet). He was being hounded by his parents' generation, and he needed the support of his peers. As Michael Cuscuna observed in *Down Beat*: "In Jim Morrison, I found, to my surprise, a beautiful human being who has been a victim of sensational publicity and harassment by silly journalists. This same Jim Morrison seems trapped in the routine of success, with a public image to live up to, while his best musical and cinematic talents and ambitions remain stifled and/or untapped." Jim himself was only too aware of the ironies of his position, caught between art and artifice, and pressured by both: "I think of myself as an intelligent, sensitive human with the soul of a clown, which always forces me to blow it at the most important moments."

The group still managed to tour in a minor-league way, paying deposits to promoters against any possible legal comeback, and usually performing under the watchful eye of the local lawmen. Apparently, it had the effect of making their set a lot tighter, and less self-indulgent – a good rock show, rather than existential catharsis. They played a few nights in Mexico City... and even Morrison was astounded by the local response to 'The End', as the audiences merrily chanted along in the Oedipal section. ('The End' was a hit single in Mexico, which says a lot about Aztec Catholicism.)

And they played two triumphant homecoming gigs at the Aquarius Theater in Los Angeles, which were recorded by Elektra for a possible live album ('Soft Parade' had made a huge loss, and a live album was one way of recouping some cash). The gigs received largely ecstatic reviews.

But for Jim Morrison, though, the joy had gone out of performing for ever: "For me, it was never really an act, those so-called performances. It was a life-and-death thing; an attempt to communicate, to involve many people in a private world of thought. I no longer feel I can best do this music through concerts. The belief isn't there."

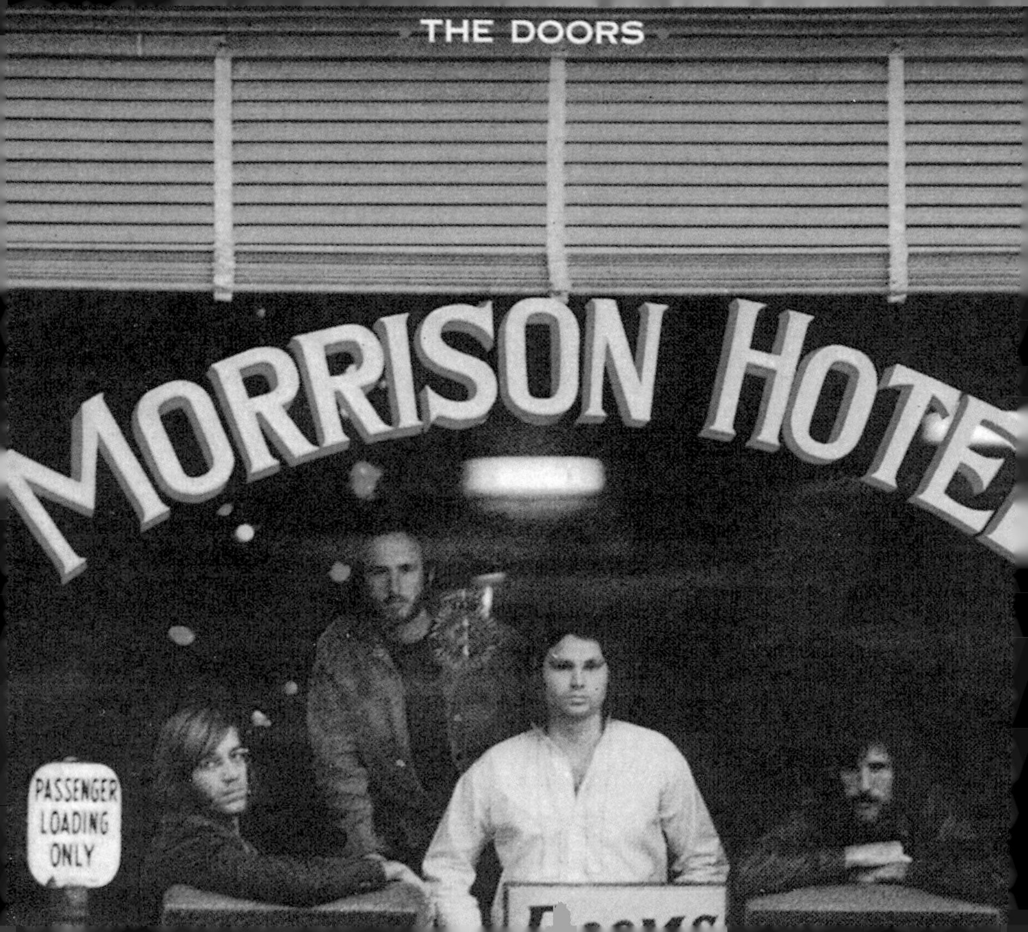
THE DOORS
MORRISON HOTE
PASSENGER LOADING ONLY

Morrison Hotel

ORIGINAL ISSUE – ELEKTRA EKS 75005

Jim was spending most of his time with Frank Lisciandro, Babe Hill and Paul Ferrara, working on the new film project, which was now titled HWY. Jim would write and co-direct, as well as act in the film. And this in turn spurred Jim to meet more people in the film world: he met with Carlos Castaneda, hoping to secure film rights to the latter's books (he was too late), talked with Steve McQueen and MGM executives about projects that would never happen.

On November 9 he returned to Miami to formally register his plea of 'Not Guilty' in court. He was released on $5,000 bail, and the trial date was set for April 1970.

But within days, Jim was in legal trouble again. He and a group of friends had decided to fly up to Phoenix to see a Rolling Stones' concert. But the party's drunken behaviour was so boisterous that the flight crew had them arrested immediately the plane touched down; under new laws designed to combat skyjacking, Jim was charged with 'interfering with the flight of an aircraft', and being drunk and disorderly (again). The charges carried a possible ten year sentence.

Elektra were still aching from the costs of 'Soft Parade', and were pushing to get the live album out as soon as possible, hopefully in time for Christmas. But the group were still taping live material; and there were still comparatively few places that would book them for gigs, so there was no way they could rush the process. So, the group did the only thing they could: they started recording a new studio album, for release as soon as possible. They were a bit battered, but somehow, The Doors had managed to survive the Sixties.

At the end of January, they played two nights at New York's Forum, previewing material from the album. Morrison spoke of the band's renewed vitality: "We started with music, then went into theatre, but it was so shitty that we went back into music, back to where we started, just being a rock band. And the music has gotten progressively better, tighter, more interesting and professional, but I think people resent that. I think they resent the fact that, when things didn't change overnight in that great renaissance of spirit, emotion and revolutionary sentiment, that we're still here doing good music."

And they were, too. In February 1970 the 'Morrison Hotel' album was released, and it was a real return to form (and certainly better than the previous two outings). *Rolling Stone* didn't like it that much, but almost everyone else did. Dave Marsh wrote in *Creem*: "The Doors have presented us with the most horrifying rock and roll I have ever heard. When they're good, they're simply unbeatable. I know this is the best record I've listened to... so far." The album took its title from the cover shot, of the band posing in the window of a sleazy skid-row hotel (which really

exists, in downtown LA); it could just as easily have been titled after the back cover shot of a working man's bar named the Hard Rock Café (which also really exists... and is there anybody out there who *doesn't* realise that this is where the burger chain took its name from?). 'Morrison Hotel' went straight to number four, staying on the charts for six months.

The reasons were simple: the band had returned to their blues roots, and junked the orchestral stuff. "We listened to 'The Soft Parade' a couple of times, and decided it would probably sound just as good without the brass," Krieger admitted in 1972. "Our music has returned to the earlier form, using just four instruments," Morrison said at the time. "We felt we'd gone too far in the other direction, i.e. orchestration, and wanted to get back to the original basic format," Jim stressed. In case no one had gotten the message, he spelt it out even more clearly: "The Doors are basically a blues-oriented band with heavy doses of rock 'n' roll, a modicum of jazz, some popular elements and a minute quantity of classical influences...

but, basically, a white blues band."

Though the album certainly has its weak moments, it has more than its fair share of strong ones: the swinging, driving 'Roadhouse Blues', which featured Giovanni Puglese (a.k.a. John Sebastian) on harmonica; the moody, bluesy strut of 'The Spy'. And Jim's writing seemed more honest, more human... and there were definitely autobiographical veins being mined: 'Peace Frog' referred to his being beaten up in New Haven, while 'Queen Of The Highway' was seemingly dedicated to Pamela. The couple had been having their problems: she had a tolerance for substance abuse almost as great as Jim's (he knew she was taking downers, but still didn't know she was shooting smack), and if he was unfaithful, so was she... and several of her affairs had seemed like they were getting serious. "I hope it can continue, just a little while longer," Jim sang sadly to his Cosmic Mate.

His legal problems continued. In March, he returned to Phoenix for a court appearance over the aeroplane incident the previ-

ous November. Despite confused testimony from one of the stewardesses, Jim was found guilty of assault (the more serious 'interference with an airline' charge was dropped). But when sentencing time came around two weeks later, the stewardess had changed her mind about Jim's involvement, and sentencing was deferred for a fortnight.

In April, *The Lords* and *The New Creatures* was published in a one-volume hardback by Simon & Schuster, which must have cheered Morrison slightly (though he hated the cover photo, and the fact that he was credited as "Jim" rather than James Douglas... but he sent a thank you note to his editor, and told Michael McClure, "This is the first time I haven't been fucked over").

The band were still recording concerts for the (now wildly overdue) live album. At a show in Boston, the auditorium's owners feared a riot, and cut the power with The Doors still on stage, much to Jim's annoyance. But they forgot to switch Jim's mike off (he called the management "cocksuckers", and told the audience "they're gonna win if you let 'em" before the band dragged him off-stage). Though nothing had really happened, the next day the group found their concert for that night had suddenly been cancelled. Which meant that they couldn't rely on live shows not falling through at the last moment. Jim was beginning to worry (and no wonder) about the way his life was going: "I'm beginning to think it's easier to scare people than to make them laugh."

But at least he got out of the Phoenix trouble; the stewardess changing her evidence resulted in all charges against him being dropped. And the Miami trial was put back until August, which at least gave Jim's lawyer Max Fink more time to prepare their case. Their initial defence notes ran to 63 pages, basing Jim's case on the concept of "contemporary social attitudes and community standards" ... i.e. trying to prove that Jim's action wouldn't seriously have outraged anybody (this was, after all, 1970). But Jim was still brooding and depressed, and

talking of retiring to Paris to write (MGM wanted him for a two-movie deal, acting and co-producing. He couldn't get excited about it).

In May, Jim was in New York, finally delivering the tapes of the live album to Elektra. While there, he began an affair with rock journalist Patricia Kennealy – nothing unusual about that, but this relationship somehow looked more serious than the others. As Kennealy later told *Rock Wives* author Victoria Balfour, "With people, he was whatever they expected him to be. Some people said he was almost kind of a mirror, just reflecting whatever you were. If you expected him to be the prince of darkness, he would oblige you... I told him once that I thought he was the shyest person that I'd ever met and that he had to create a sensation as a sort of cover up. He said that was just incredibly perceptive and very mean of me to say so."

Kennealy was a practising Wiccan witch, and the head of a coven ("It's not Satanism. It's basically a mother religion, but there is also a god figure, a horned god of the hunt"), all of which deeply intrigued Morrison. Later that month, he stopped off in New York en route to Europe, to see her again. The first night he came down with a fever, and his temperature reached 105 degrees; it broke just as suddenly. The following night, he suggested they get 'married' in a Wiccan wedding ceremony, and she agreed. Clad in black robes and standing inside a magical circle, the couple were 'married' by a high priest and priestess of the Celtic coven in Kennealy's apartment on Midsummer's Night 1970. Jim passed out when he had to sign his name in blood.

But for her, it was definitely love: "If T.S. Eliot had been a rock group, he would have been The Doors and done 'The Soft Parade'," she wrote in one review (love alone might explain why she picked their worst album to get pretentious about). The relationship didn't last, however, the final straw coming later that year, when Kennealy discovered she was pregnant. In the middle of Jim's Miami trial, he and Kennealy agreed that she should have an abortion. "Maybe it had

something to do with the twenty paternity suits against him," she later said. Though they remained in touch until shortly before Jim departed the States for good, their relationship was never the same again.

Jim left for Europe a few days after his 'wedding', in largely optimistic mood (apart from Patricia, the MGM deal now looked a lot less idiotic and a lot more promising – and those in the industry who had seen the now completed *HWY* had been impressed). He flew to Paris, where he went sightseeing for a week, before heading down to Spain and North Africa for another two weeks. He returned to the States in time for the release of the live album; and promptly collapsed with pneumonia – his second bout of serious illness in a matter of months. He put it down to walking in the European rain too much; but though he appeared to recover quickly, he was in truth far more sick than anybody near him could begin to guess.

ABSOLUTELY LIVE

the doors

Absolutely Live

ORIGINAL ISSUE – ELEKTRA 2665 002

When 'Absolutely Live' finally appeared, nobody was too surprised that it was a double album (they'd been all the vogue in '68 and '69), and that it contained a number of new songs (the most important being the full version of 'Celebration Of The Lizard'). It had been recorded at concerts in LA, Philadelphia and New York, and it had taken a heck of a time to get finished (Densmore confessed in 1977: "Getting the live album to work, and doing it, took a lot longer than we'd thought, so it came out a lot later than we'd all wanted. We wanted to do it a lot earlier").

So, was it worth the wait? Frankly, no. Not that it's *particularly* bad, though it certainly has its rough spots ('When The Music's Over', and 'Break On Through'); but the main problem is that of Jim's audience interaction... which may have been inspiring on the night, but if so, then you truly had to have been there. The album is basically of interest almost solely for 'Lizard', which is at least adventurous and experimental, on the downside, It ain't exactly choc full of toe-tapping hits. Good version of 'Soul Kitchen', though.

Morrison was at least honest about the album: "I think it's a true document of one of our good concerts. It's not insanely good, but it's a true portrait of what we usually do on a good night." It entered the charts the day Jim flew to Miami, to finally face the music.

It took two days just to select the jury... and as the *LA.Free Press* noted, "Jurors in Florida, although half in number, are apparently twice as good as elsewhere. They are also twice as old; the youngest juror is forty-two, the rationale apparently being that anyone under the age of thirty is necessarily prejudiced." Jim's counsel

objected to the jury, pointing out that they could hardly be said to be Morrison's peer group. The objection was ignored by Judge Murray Goodman, who was up for election later that year, and throughout the trial, it was clear to most onlookers that Jim was a young man being hounded by older men, a martyr to the fabled 'generation gap'. It turned out that Robert Jennings – who had brought the charge against Morrison, and who asserted that Jim had flashed his genitalia for "between five and eight seconds" – was an employee of the state attorney. And Goodman seemingly had a grudge against Jim's Florida lawyer, Bob Josefsberg. The jury were read a supposed transcript of Jim's in-concert banter, some of which is priceless (and almost certainly inaccurate): "Take your fucking friend and love him. Do you want to see my cock?"

Court adjourned for several days, allowing The Doors to play two concerts in California. It can't have been much of a respite for Morrison, who was also having to deal with the matter of Patricia Kennealy's pregnancy. When it recon-

vened, Jim's attorney Max Fink was soon given a rude shock. Fink had been basing their defence on the concept of 'community standards', and was all for taking the jury to see *Hair* and *Woodstock*, so they could judge Jim in that cultural context. Judge Goodman was having none of it, and threw the concept out of court. Fink protested; Goodman wouldn't budge. There went their defence.

The trial went on. Four policemen testified they'd heard Morrison talking dirty and making obscene gestures. The defence agreed to the playing of a tape of the concert, hoping that at least the jury would be able to judge Jim's words for themselves; by the time the tape finished playing, they probably knew they'd made a mistake.

Court adjourned again, allowing The Doors to travel to play at the third Isle Of Wight Festival in England (they'd had to cancel a planned European tour, because of the trial). I saw them play, and (despite the dodgy sound) thoroughly enjoyed their set (though many – including Jim – thought they weren't that great that night). Backstage, Morrison pleaded tiredness and jet lag, commented on festival culture and the 'Woodstock generation' ("Even though they can be a mess and might not be what they pretend to be, it's still better than nothing, and I'm sure some of the people take away a kind of myth back to the city with them, and it'll affect them"); he talked of starting his own magazine ("a manifesto, like the Surrealists and Dadaists used to put out"), and claimed he'd just made his last live appearance. Three days later, he was back in court in Miami.

When the court reconvened, the prosecution rested its case. There was little the defence could do but parade a dozen witnesses, who all said they hadn't seen Jim do anything. But it was their word against that of the prosecution witnesses, and Jim must have known they didn't stand much of a chance.

When the verdict came in, Jim was found innocent of lewd behaviour and drunkenness (which was ironic; Morrison had even admitted to being drunk on the witness stand), but guilty of profanity. As regards indecent exposure, the jury were undecided... until the following day, when they declared Jim to be guilty.

Sentencing would take place in October. In the meantime, bail was set at $50,000 – a phenomenal amount in the circumstances, from which it would seem that the Miami authorities were determined to see Jim in jail, however briefly. Totally unfazed, Fink wrote out a cheque for the amount, and The Doors' party immediately left town.

(Apparently, it's true to say that Jim's privates *did* get exposed in Miami: on one of the return trips connected with the trial Morrison partied hard one night with old friends Creedence Clearwater Revival. Jim passed out and was laid out on their suite's pool table, which they then surrounded with candles, as if the 'corpse' were lying in state. As a parting gesture, they fished out the Morrison member that had so outraged Miami, and left Jim lying there. Legend has it that the group checked out the next morning, leaving the spectacle to be discovered by a squealing chambermaid.)

Morrison was, understandably, deeply depressed. Jimi Hendrix died the day he heard the Miami verdict. Janis Joplin died a couple of weeks later. Jim supposedly told his bar-room buddies, "You're drinking with number three." He picked a fight with Pamela, and she left him, flying to Paris to join a French lover. And on October 30, Jim Morrison was in the Miami courtroom again. In the gap between verdict and sentencing he'd been interviewed by *Circus* magazine; he was defiant, but obviously depressed, about the future; he seemed to believe he was truly facing a prison sentence: "This trial, and its outcome, won't change my style, because I maintain that I didn't do anything wrong. It's actually a very fascinating thing to go through, a thing you can observe. If I have to go to jail, I hope the others will go on and create an instrumental sound of their own, one that doesn't depend on lyrics. Lyrics aren't really that essential in music, anyhow."

Judge Goodman told him, "The suggestion that your conduct was acceptable by community standards is just not true. To admit that this nation accepts as a community standard the indecent exposure and the offensive language spoken by you would be to admit that a small minority who spew obscenities, who disregard law and order, and who display utter contempt for our institutions and heritage have determined the community standards for us all." Jim was sunk, the Judge gave him the maximum possible sentence: a $500 fine, and sixty days hard labour in a Florida jail for the profanity, and another six months hard labour for the exposure. But he'd never serve his time.

DOORS

L.A.WOMAN

L A Woman

ORIGINAL ISSUE – ELEKTRA K-42090

In November 1970, within two weeks of Jim's sentencing, Max Fink filed an appeal with the U.S. District Court to have the convictions quashed.

Meanwhile, Elektra – disappointed with the poor sales of the live album (a mere 225,000 copies shifted) – decided to release a Doors 'greatest hits' compilation entitled '13', to make the most of all of the publicity and scoop up some Christmas cash. The Doors were appalled. They struck back the only way they could – by rehearsing material for a new album, the last they owed Elektra under the terms of their contract. But, after attending a few rehearsals, Paul Rothchild told them he didn't want to produce the new album: "Jim especially was really bored... couldn't really get himself up for it. I said, 'This album is going to be a disaster.' One moment, I just got up, went into the studio and said, 'Hey, listen – I'm bored. First time in my life when I've been in the studio that I've had my head down on the console. I love you guys, and I love the music, but it seems to me that you're doing nothing to me and I'm doing nothing to you. I want both our careers to survive, so why don't you go on and produce yourselves?'"

As Krieger recalled in 1972: "It was a mutual thing, really. We found out that after four or five albums, a group learns how to get what they want in the studio, and Paul didn't really have anything more to say that we didn't already think of ourselves, so he wasn't really a necessary factor anymore. He didn't feel he was contributing enough to be the producer. He's one of those producers who really has to get his whole trip into the thing, put his whole energy into it, into what he's doing... and this time, we knew what *we* wanted."

They decided to produce the album themselves, with engineer Bruce Botnick's help... and to keep the whole project close to home, they had the rehearsal room under The Doors' office converted into a recording studio, with a recording console and tape deck in the upper offices.

Manzarek explained their attitude in 1972: "It was back to basics, back to the roots. We brought microphones and recording equipment right into the rehearsal room. Instead of using a professional studio, we said 'Hey, let's record this album where we rehearse and let's have a spontaneous, live kinda feel.' We brought Jerry Scheff in on bass and Marc Benno on rhythm guitar – we'd never used a rhythm guitar player before – so we had six musicians all going at the same time. 'LA Woman' is a live take – Jim sang the song while we played it. There were very few overdubs, an absolute minimum. I think I overdubbed a tack piano on 'LA Woman'... and that's about it. Everything else was an actual live recording, as if it were done on stage. That's why it sounds so fresh."

They'd returned to recording more or less the same way they'd done their first album, with very few overdubs (much to Jim's relief). Some of the vocals for the album were recorded in the bathroom at The Doors' studio on 8512 Santa Monica Boulevard – hence the jokey line on 'Hyacinth House': "I see the bathroom is clear" – a lyric which would assume spooky significance within a year.

But Jim's voice often sounds tired and shot, almost at breaking point... and ironically, if anything, that only adds to the raw blues feel of it all. This album took them further down the road they'd started with 'Morrison Hotel', and on much better form. Jim knew it, too; the fact that all the songs are credited to The Doors as a group once again (for the first time since their third album) shows that he was comfortable with both the material and with his companions. "At last, I'm doing a blues album," he told friends enthusiastically. Strangely, the weakest track – a lacklustre version of John Lee Hooker's

'Crawling King Snake' – had been a concert staple since their earliest gigs.

According to Robbie Krieger, 'The Wasp (Texas Radio & The Big Beat)' is about: "The new music Jim heard when his family moved around the Southwest States. He'd got this vision of a huge radio tower spewing out noise. This was when XERB was broadcasting and Wolfman Jack was on the air. You could hear the Wolfman from Tijuana and Tallahassee up to Chicago, where Ray Manzarek lived. That started rock'n'roll for our generation. It was black polished chrome and there were no laws then about how powerful a radio station could be."

Title track 'LA Woman' was an ode to a woman, or the city of the angels, or both (Morrison had stolen the image "city of night" from a novel by John Rechy); it didn't much matter, it was so hypnotic... and against the darkness of his vision, Morrison exhorted "Mr Mojo Risin'" (this being an anagram of Jim Morrison that had been discovered by John Sebastian), i.e. *himself* to "keep on risin'".

The album closed with 'Riders On The Storm', a bluesy dream of the apocalypse which was adapted by Morrison from a stoned telephone conversation he'd had with a friend. It was also part of a poem entitled 'The Graveyard'... though the "Killer on the road" section was taken from the script to Morrison's movie *HWY*. Bruce Botnick added the sounds of a rainstorm and a howling train (the band wanted to add horses' hooves riding across a metal bridge as well). Rothchild later dismissed it as "cocktail music" (one wonders what kind of cocktails *he* was used to !)

Jim told the *NME*'s Roy Carr earlier in the year that he fantasised about The Doors recording with blues giants like Muddy Waters and John Lee Hooker: "It would be like something you've never heard before. Maybe one day it will happen! There's no reason why it shouldn't. Bring in people like Hooker, Screamin' Jay Hawkins... even somebody like Lee Dorsey; not just to cover a bunch of old familiar blues songs, but to write new material. We used to perform Dorsey's 'Get Out My Life Woman' and a bunch of

that stuff. A Doors' blues album would surprise a lot of people."

They never did get to record with their blues forefathers, but at least they'd recorded a great album (their *greatest*, thought *Rolling Stone*), probably little realising that it would be their last. Jim Morrison did re-enter a recording studio on one occasion, though – on his 27th birthday, to lay down on tape a reading of his poetry (which, almost all his friends agree, was meant to be heard rather than read). He taped for hours (including a reading of *An American Prayer*, a new

work he'd had privately printed in a limited edition of 500 copies), and during the session he got slowly drunk... but when it was over he was highly pleased, and evidently felt he'd achieved some personal goal. On an 'up', he agreed to play live with The Doors again, and two dates were quickly set up, in Dallas and New Orleans.

But Morrison was worn out – drugs, booze, the stress of living with the Miami sentence hanging over him (not to mention a flock of paternity suits) and general physical illness were all taking their toll. The Dallas gig went fine – they previewed 'Riders On The Storm', and the crowd loved it – but in New Orleans The Doors' stage career came to an end. Manzarek later remarked: "Anybody who was there that night saw it. Jim just... lost all his energy halfway into the set. You could almost see it leave him; he hung onto the mike stand and his spirit just slipped away. He was finally drained, I guess." Frustrated by his failing body, Jim repeatedly smashed the mike stand into the stage floor, before slumping down motionless on the drum riser. He never performed on a concert stage anywhere again.

There was some good news: Elektra were interested in the poetry tapes for possible release, and Simon & Schuster were planning a paperback of *The Lords* and *The New Creatures*. But it was time to go. Pam had returned to him, and he'd decided to go back to Paris with her. Though exile would be hard for him (he once stated, "I am primarily an American; second, a Californian; third, a resident of Los Angeles"), he probably believed that living in Paris would give him the fresh start he needed; away from the American courts and the American media, in the atmosphere that had inspired other American writers like Hemingway and F. Scott Fitzgerald. Surely in Paris, he'd be able to concentrate on his serious writing.

As Manzarek tells it: "Jim left for Paris right in the middle of the mixing of 'LA Woman' – I think we had two more songs to mix – and he said, 'Hey man, everything's going fine here. Why don't you guys finish it up? Pam and I are going to

Paris, and we're just going to hang out for a while, see what happens.' So we said, 'Okay, talk to you later. Go over there and have a good time, relax, take it easy. Write some poetry.'

"What Jim wanted to do in leaving for Paris was to immerse himself in an artistic environment, to get away from Los Angeles, to get away from rock'n'roll, to get away from all the sensational press that he had. Jim was hounded by a lot of sensational press; a lot of yellow journalism associated with the man and, frankly, he was tired of it. He was tired of being 'The Lizard King'. Jim Morrison was a poet. He was an artist. He didn't want to be the king of orgasmic rock, the king of acid rock, the Lizard King. He felt all those titles that people had put on him were demeaning to what The Doors were trying to do, so in an attempt to escape that, and to recharge his artistic batteries, he went to Paris, the city of art. He was going to write, maybe look into a few film projects – Agnes Varda had contacted him about doing a movie, as had Jacques Demis.

"So Jim was just getting away, taking a

breather, a rest... going to become a poet again. And we had finished our commitment to Elektra; we had to deliver seven records over that five or six year period of time. So we had completed our contract, and were free to go to a new record company, continue making records, *not* make records, whatever. So, we decided to just take a long hiatus, and there was really no reason for Jim to be there for the mix. He said, 'You guys finish it up, I'm going to Paris.' We said, 'Okay man, see you later'... and I haven't heard from him since."

Before leaving Los Angeles for Paris that March, Morrison had asked the other Doors, 'What would happen to you if I died?' Were these morbid presentiments, or was (as many would like to believe) Morrison planning to fake his death? Or was it just idle curiosity? He had good reason to want to disappear, certainly; it was a lot more appealing than jail.

The truth is probably a lot simpler, and less romantic: Jim Morrison was desperately ill, and he knew it. A year earlier, he'd discovered cocaine, and had – as was usual with Jim and substances – consumed large quantities of it. According to Robby Krieger, Jim was in pretty poor shape, and had been coughing up blood even before he left Los Angeles.

In Paris he joined Pamela at the Hotel de Nice, in the rue des Beaux Arts, where they lived for three weeks before moving to 17 rue Beautreillis, close to the centre of Paris. Only a few friends knew he was in Paris. He shaved off his trademark heavy beard, but was still pretty chubby. In April 'LA Woman' was released (to general critical acclaim), but in Paris Jim was practically unknown, could walk the streets unmolested by fans or journalists. Back in LA, the other Doors bided their time, waiting for the call from Jim which they were sure would one day come. "We'd rehearse once in a while... maybe get together twice a week, working on some songs and stuff, and just waiting for Jim to come back." And he did call a couple of times, just to say 'hi'.

As the months passed, Morrison began to relax, as the pressures of rock star life slipped away from him. He and Pamela went on short trips to Spain,

Morocco, and Corsica, as well as other areas of France. But he hadn't been able to focus on writing at all, and when he tried to arrange Parisian screenings of *Feast Of Friends* and *HWY*, he met with little interest. He spent most of his time hanging out with the half-dozen people he and Pam knew in Paris; and he was still drinking prodigiously (though he was now aware that his problem with alcohol was a serious one, and was supposedly attempting to cut down on his intake), and still occasionally using cocaine. But he'd coughed up blood on several occasions now, and was noticeably out of breath after climbing stairs. He had coughing fits at night, and consulted a doctor, who prescribed pills for asthma (according to Pamela, he'd also seen a doctor in London regarding the same problem). But Jim didn't like doctors (his earlier bouts of pneumonia hadn't been treated properly), and wouldn't take medicines.

Then, in the early hours of Saturday July 3, 1971, the brief, tragic life of James Douglas Morrison (poet) came to an end. He'd dined out the night before, then tak-en Pamela to a late movie before returning to their flat and going to bed about 2.30 a.m. An hour or so later, Pamela had been woken by Jim's erratic and noisy breathing – she thought that he was choking, and woke him. He refused her pleas that they should call a doctor, and said that he'd decided to have a bath. Then, according to Pamela's police statement :
"When he was in the bath he called me and said that he felt sick and felt like vomiting. On my way I picked up an orange coloured bowl. He vomited food into the bowl I was holding. I think there was blood in it. I emptied the contents then my friend vomited into the container again, only blood this time, and then a third time blood clots. Each time I emptied the bowl down the wash basin of the bathroom, then I washed the bowl. My friend then told me he felt strange but he said, 'I don't feel sick, don't call a doctor, I feel better. It's over !' He told me to 'go to bed', and said that he was going to finish his bath and would join me in bed. At this time it appeared to me that my friend felt better because he had vomited and his colour

had returned a bit. I went back to bed and immediately fell asleep. I was reassured."

Some hours later Pamela awoke with a start to discover that Jim hadn't returned to bed, and discovered his body lying in the tepid bath water. A little blood had trickled from his nose, and he was smiling.

At first Pamela thought Jim was playing a sick joke on her – then she decided that he was unconscious. Unable to rouse him, or lift him out of the bath, she called a friend, Alan Ronay, who arrived at the Morrison's apartment with his girlfriend Agnes Varda (though neither of them saw the body). Either Pamela or Ronay had called the emergency services, and the first to arrive were the fire brigade resuscitation unit, followed shortly thereafter by the police. But Jim was beyond any help they may have offered. He was pronounced dead, of natural causes due to a heart attack, aged 27. Though the body was not examined by the Police Doctor until over twelve hours after death, the police did not deem an autopsy necessary.

Pamela made a statement to the police (which contained the intriguing comment, "my boyfriend was a writer, but mostly he lived on a personal fortune"). Inevitably, rumours of Jim's death leaked out almost immediately, and by July 5 the rumours had reached Los Angeles. Since 'Jim is dead' rumours were not only nothing new but decidedly old hat, Bill Siddons wasn't particularly worried. But, unable to confirm or deny the report with Parisian police and the American Embassy, Siddons finally called Pam. She told him that something had happened to Jim, but refused to give any details. Fearing the worst, Siddons immediately flew to Paris, where he was confronted at the Morrison's apartment by Pamela, a death certificate and a sealed coffin. He never saw (or asked to see) the body; and this fact - coupled with the earlier denial of Jim's death by the Parisian police - led to the popular rumours that Jim (like James Dean and Elvis) had perhaps faked his own death, and escaped to the highways of myth. When Pamela died of a heroin overdose three years later, she took whatever secrets she had with her to the grave.

Morrison had once said he'd like to die "at about 120 with a sense of humour and a nice comfy bed." Given Jim's habits, this option had never seemed that likely. One wonders if he was granted another, earlier wish: "I don't want to die in my sleep, or of old age, or O.D. ... I want to feel what it's like. I want to taste it, hear it, smell it. Death is only going to happen to you once; I don't want to miss it."

At 9.00am on Wednesday July 7th, Jim's mortal remains were buried in the Parisian cemetery of Père Lachaise, where the remains of (amongst others) Oscar Wilde, Edith Piaf and Chopin are also interred. No clergyman was present, nor were any members of Jim's family or the other Doors. The only mourners were Pam, Bill Siddons, Alan Ronay and Agnes Varda, and another American friend living in Paris, Robin Wertle.

Pam and Siddons spent the next day going through Jim's belongings and packing, then flew directly to Los Angeles, where Bill announced the news of Jim's death to the world: "I have just returned from Paris, where I attended the funeral of Jim Morrison. Jim was buried in a simple ceremony, with only a few friends present.

"The initial news of his death and funeral was kept quiet because those of us who knew him intimately and loved him as a person wanted to avoid all the notoriety and circus-like atmosphere that surrounded the deaths of such other rock personalities as Janis Joplin and Jimi Hendrix.

"I can say that Jim died peacefully of natural causes – he had been in Paris since March with his wife, Pam. He had seen a doctor in Paris about a respiratory problem, and had complained of this problem on Saturday – the day of his death.

"I hope that Jim is remembered not only as a rock singer and poet, but as a warm human being. He was the most warm, most human, most understanding person I've known. That wasn't always the Jim Morrison people read about – but it was the Jim Morrison I knew and his close friends will remember..."

AN AMERICAN PRAYER

JIM MORRISON

MUSIC BY

THE DOORS

Other Voices, full circle & an American Prayer

When Jim died I thought 'Shit! What do I do now?'" Krieger later recalled. "All I had ever known was music. I couldn't fathom the idea of doing anything else." Though Jim's trip to Paris had meant putting The Doors on indefinite hold, none of the band had expected that the group would never reform. Especially for such a dramatic reason – John Densmore later said the group were all "shocked beyond belief. That really did it... we just thought, 'What now?' We sat around, and then we jammed a bit, and finally we decided to keep the music going, keep on making music. The vibes between the three of us had been so good that we felt we just had to continue. Jim was a friend, somebody you'd lived with and made music with for so long, but eventually we began to realise that we had the rest of our lives to live. So, after we'd gotten over it, we started to think about what we'd do. None of us really wanted to go play with anyone else, so after five years of being together and getting tighter, we decided to start the whole thing again."

"As Manzarek recalled in 1972: "At first, we were very unsure of ourselves – we didn't know exactly what we were going to sound like. We knew that the music would be OK, but we weren't too sure about the vocals, how they were gonna sound. We didn't know how it was going to gel... but little by little, it all began falling together."

The remaining Doors debated changing their name, but decided against it ("no one could come up with anything that didn't sound real pretentious," Krieger later admitted). They also decided not to attempt to replace Jim, but to tackle the vocals themselves. As Ray explained, "Yes, we thought about finding another singer, but it seemed kinda impossible to bring in another personality... and what if he wasn't the right guy? And, of course, it would be really hard on him too, because he'd always be Jim's replacement."

So the group entered The Doors' Workshop in July 1971, and began work on songs (including rejects and leftovers from 'LA Woman') for a forthcoming album. Bruce Botnick produced, and the vocals were tackled mainly by Ray, with Robbie singing harmonies, and lead on a couple of tracks; in addition, five bassists and two percussionists rounded out the sound. The result, the 'Other Voices' album, released in December 1971, was a good deal better than many people expected... but Morrison's absence, lyrically and vocally, left too big a hole to fill. Though the album reached 31 on the U.S. charts, most listeners and reviewers agreed with *Rolling Stone*: "It is Doors music mainly due to its trappings... they are still The Doors, but without a cause or passion; it is obvious that Jim Morrison was more than just a singer..."

"I think it's going to take people a little while to adjust to what we're doing," Manzarek pointed out. "At first, I think it

might be rather confusing for them... but little by little, if they'll just listen and dig the music... "

At least the concert audiences were enthusiastic, as the trio (plus bassist Jack Conrad and percussionist rhythm guitarist Bobby Ray) toured Canada and the States that winter to promote the album (to general critical acclaim). In the spring of 1972, they headed for Europe, playing dates in Germany, Switzerland, France, Belgium, Holland and the UK, finishing the tour with a concert at Imperial College, London, before returning to LA to begin work on the next album.

The sessions didn't work out well. They abandoned The Doors Workshop for A&M's Hollywood studio, and also dropped producer Bruce Botnick. This time the guest musicians included respected jazz flute and sax player Charles Lloyd, and the proceedings as a whole had a much jazzier – and disconnected – feel. The finished album, 'Full Circle', was released in September 1972. Adding its own flaws to the faults of the previous outing, the results are generally dismal. It peaked at number 68 on the U.S. charts, and this time the critics felt no need to pull punches at all. "I've had trouble getting past Side one," admitted *Creem* reviewer Buck Sanders. "In fact, I don't *care* about getting past Side one..."

"In retrospect, 'Full Circle' was a bit of a disaster," Densmore admitted later, "but at the time, we had our hearts in it. Then, about halfway through, the songwriting thing started to get on everyone's nerves. Which song are we going to do? Ray's turning this way, Robbie's going that way, so it all got a little bit touchy, which is why I don't think our album turned out all that well." Krieger's hindsight view of the post-Jim albums is even blunter: "We hoped to capture something, but it never felt very good. Without him it was very awkward. There was no balance any more. We were totally fucked."

They hadn't admitted it yet, though. But they all knew that, if they were to continue, something had to be done in the vocal department: they needed a proper lead singer. In autumn 1972 they travelled to London to audition vocalists. (Why London? Who knows?) For Manzarek, the experience was an unhappy one, and he soon decided that enough was enough. He announced he was quitting, and flew home to LA. As he recalled later: "We wanted to recharge our creative batteries, just as Jim did when he went to Paris... but it didn't really work out. It was time to close The Doors."

Manzarek eventually got a solo deal, with Mercury Records. The first fruit of this was 1974's jazz-rock outing 'The Golden Scarab' ("dizzily pretentious", according to the *NME*). The following year he released another (rockier)album, 'The Whole Thing Started With Rock 'N' Roll, Now It's Out Of Control', which boasted guest shots from Flo & Eddie and poetess Patti Smith (reading from *The New Creatures*) and is thus *slightly* more interesting. Both albums were released on Mercury.

Meanwhile, John and Robbie had stayed in London, persevering in their quest for a singer, though Densmore totally understood Ray's reasons for leaving: "Everyone, myself included, was writing songs, and all of Ray's were real personal, and so it finally got to the point where it was obvious that he was the only one who could sing them, because they'd be very philosophical and cosmic or whatever – so how could another singer relate to material that was so personal? So, when we first came over, we were still together – sort of – but when we realised how very differently our musical directions were heading, Ray split back home. Then Robbie and I decided that, as we'd come over to start something new, we might as well do it anyway. And so, for the next four months or so, we lived here and jammed with different people, and eventually sorted something out."

Kevin Coyne, Howard Werth and Jess Roden were all considered as possible vocalists (it's rumoured they also considered Iggy Pop, who supposedly dyed his hair black just in case...), and they settled on Roden. They called their new group The Butts Band, recruiting Phillip Chen on keyboards and Roy Davies on

bass, with Roden on vocals, and commenced rehearsing and recording in early 1973. Their (fairly dull) début album – 1974's 'The Butts Band' – was partly recorded in Jamaica, and the *NME* called the reggae-influenced results "marginally promising". But – not wanting to up sticks for L.A. – Roden left after a short U.K. tour, and the band – strained to the limit by the fact that Krieger and Densmore lived on a different continent to the others – fell apart. The following year Densmore and Krieger tried again, with a new Butts Band: Michael Stull on vocals and guitar, Alex Richman on keyboards, Mike Berkowitz on drums and Karl Ruckner on bass. But the resultant album ('Hear And Now') got even worse reviews, and the band broke up shortly after. Both albums were released on Blue Thumb Records (the first released on Island in the U.K.)

In 1976, Manzarek resurfaced with a new band, Nite City – they lasted until late '77 and produced two albums before they split (bassist Nigel Harrison ended up in Blondie) – the first was big in LA (but nowhere else), the second only got

released in Germany. And in 1977, after a period of seeming inactivity, Krieger also reappeared, fronting his own jazz-rock outfit. They recorded one album – 'Robby Krieger & Friends' – on the jazz label Blue Note. Though all three Doors continue to make the occasional appearance on record to this day, they now have other concerns: Densmore has for some years been pursuing an acting career, while Manzarek moved into production (the most successful act he's signed to date was LA band X), forming a production and management company with former Doors' office helper Danny Sugerman (of whom we shall hear more shortly).

But Jim's ghost still hovered at their shoulder, and whatever the surviving Doors had attempted or achieved, it seemed Morrison's shadow would always fall across them. It was time they dealt with it... though ironically the means would concern the one aspect of Jim's work that he always tried to keep separate from his Doors persona – his poetry. (The day before he died, Morrison had telegrammed his editor at Simon & Schuster, who were about to publish *The Lords* and *The New Creatures* in a collected, mass market edition, about a proposed cover change. Legend has it that

Morrison wanted both his photo and any mention of The Doors removed from the cover. One doubts they would have agreed to the alterations.)

Morrison had recorded several hours worth of his recited poetry before his death, but the tapes had never been released. Eventually, the fact niggled and surfaced noisily from John Densmore's memory: "So I called up John Haney, who engineered the sessions and asked, 'What happened to Jim's poetry tapes? Do you have any copies?' The guy said, 'Better than that, I have the originals. Why don't you and the other guys come over? We can listen to them, see if there's anything there, and maybe we could do something with them.' And that's how it all got started."

Rumours began to surface that the ex-Doors were working on the project together, and in the summer of 1977, John Densmore confirmed it: "We've been researching these damned poems for about a year or so, but the last few months we've been getting serious, meeting a couple of times a week. Hopefully, in the next two or three months we'll get into it five days a week, wrap it up and have it out for Christmas but... you see, this is *our* idea. It's not one of your Jimi Hendrix fourth album after he's died kind of thing, jamming in the background with some fat jazz sax player; nor is it a case of the record company going back into the files, digging out some old tapes and putting them out with a new jacket. This is Jim's poetry album – he never got to finish it, so now Ray, Robbie and I are doing it for him. It's not going to be a straight blah, blah, blah, nothing straight through for ten minutes or whatever. It's going to be like a biography: his childhood, teenage years, young man, public life. It was all done on a 16-track, so we're gonna write some new music under the poems, and we'll have a little bit of old stuff to tie it all together, plus some real nice stories he tells about when he was making his films, various things in his life. They make it kinda biographical, and so it has a little theme. It's Jim's life, really."

The project proved a difficult one, as

Jim wasn't around to do re-takes; they had to work with what they'd got. "Jim's getting back at us," said Densmore. "This time, it's like he's saying, 'OK, now it's *your* turn to do the overdubs!" In the end, Densmore's prediction of a Christmas 1977 release date for the album proved wildly optimistic. "We ran into snags," Manzarek later admitted, while Krieger added: "The fact is, that this album is so revolutionary in the way we had to make it that we really shouldn't have projected dates. There was no way to tell how long something was going to take... it turned out that for everything we said, 'OK, this shouldn't take more than a month, it took about three months." As Manzarek explained, "We had no models to work from, because a record like this had never been made before."

'An American Prayor' was finally released in November 1978. It was credited to Jim Morrison, with "Music by The Doors" receiving only slightly less cover acreage. None of the poetry contained within had been seen or heard before, with the exception of the title track, which had been published in a limited edition of 500 copies. As Manzarek explained, they'd included the piece because so few people had seen it: "'An American Prayer' was a private edition that Jim handed out to friends and certain fans, and over the years I've had many people come up to me and ask, 'How do I get a copy of it? I've heard about it and want to read it.' So naturally, we thought it would have to be included on the album. It was so good, we felt it belonged in a larger scope than just 500 copies out there somewhere."

Manzarek concluded: "I hope the people who are going to listen to this album will perceive that it's quite a unique experience... it's not something to put on while you're doing the dishes, or mending the car. You have to put this record on, sit down and listen. It demands. All it asks for is 40 minutes of your time, and if you'll give those 40 minutes, we'll take you somewhere that maybe you've never been before."

And it's certainly an interesting addition to The Doors canon – almost giving the feel of a lengthy improvisation. But while the backing might have made Jim's poetry more commercially acceptable and brought it to a larger audience than it might otherwise have had, it also made it even harder to distinguish between Morrison the poet and Morrison the Doors' lyricist. And it ain't *that* commercial – as Manzarek, pointed out, it's scarcely background music. But most critics felt the project was a worthy one, and gave the results an almost unanimous thumbs up.

But what of the poetry? At his worst ("Death and my cock are the world"), Morrison is just plain embarrassing; at his best he has genuine humour, insight and power... the more so for hearing him recite his own work. Even in his poetry, Morrison was a *performer*. Reviewing the album for *Creem*, rock poetess Patti Smith (who'd learnt a trick or two from Jim herself) wrote: "In biblical times he may have appeared as Moses or Samson or his pick of mad prophets. Today the drama of his intensity seems dated. Dated in its passion and innocence, like *West Side Story* or *The Grapes Of Wrath*. But he was always dated, at his most literal, even when he was around. Bigger than life and so he was laughable. Laughed at by the court, but loved by the people."

Though previously unpublished Morrison poetry has since appeared via Frank Lisciandro (*A Feast Of Friends*) and via Pamela Courson's family (*Wilderness : The Lost Writings* and *The American Night: Lost Writings Vol.11*), it's worth bearing in mind that – along with the 500-copy run of *An American Prayer* – *The Lords* and *The New Creatures* is the only collection Morrison himself approved. When these books were first (privately) printed, Jim was reported to have said, "Now I can die happy."

One bonus for Doors fans was the inclusion on 'An American Prayer' of a previously unreleased live version of 'Roadhouse Blues', and the admission that there was at least one other track ('Gloria') in the vaults. And the album had used up only a tiny percentage (less than

10%) of the poetry tapes Jim had recorded, so a follow-up wasn't out of the question (unless the other tapes were substandard, or otherwise unusable); its success certainly convinced Manzarek for one that there was indeed a market out there for unreleased Doors material. He hinted that their next project would be a full-length Doors documentary: "We have 50,000 feet or so of footage of The Doors. That's lurking in the wings, very possibly one of the next projects... but the reason why it's lurking is that, like this album, if it's done, it's going to be done properly." Fifteen years on, the project is presumably still "lurking".

But – even though it was nominated for a Best Spoken Word Grammy Award (it didn't win) – not everyone thought 'An American Prayer' *had* been "done properly" – Paul Rothchild dismissed the album as "a rape. In my mind, what they did to 'An American Prayer' was on a par with taking a painting by Picasso, cutting it up into hundreds of small pieces and spreading it across a supermarket wall. It was the first commercial sell-out of Jim Morrison." It wouldn't be the last...

But the next Doors item to surface was similarly interesting. In 1979 Francis Ford Coppola finally completed his epic Vietnam movie, *Apocalypse Now*. Coppola had long wanted to have Doors' music present in the movie – he'd even approached Manzarek about composing an original soundtrack, but the idea came to nothing (he'd also shot a scene – cut from the final version of the movie – in which Marlon Brando as Kurtz teaches his primitive native army the lyrics to 'Light My Fire' !). Finally, Coppola settled for opening and closing his film with The Doors' original recording of 'The End'; remixing the song for the movie, Coppola discovered on the master tape the vocal part which Paul Rothchild had (deliberately) buried in the mix back in 1967: "During the whole big raga thing, Jim's going 'kill, kill, kill', and at another point he's going 'fuck, fuck, fuck' as a rhythm instrument..." The *Apocalypse Now* soundtrack was *also* nominated for the Best Spoken Word Grammy. It didn't win either ...

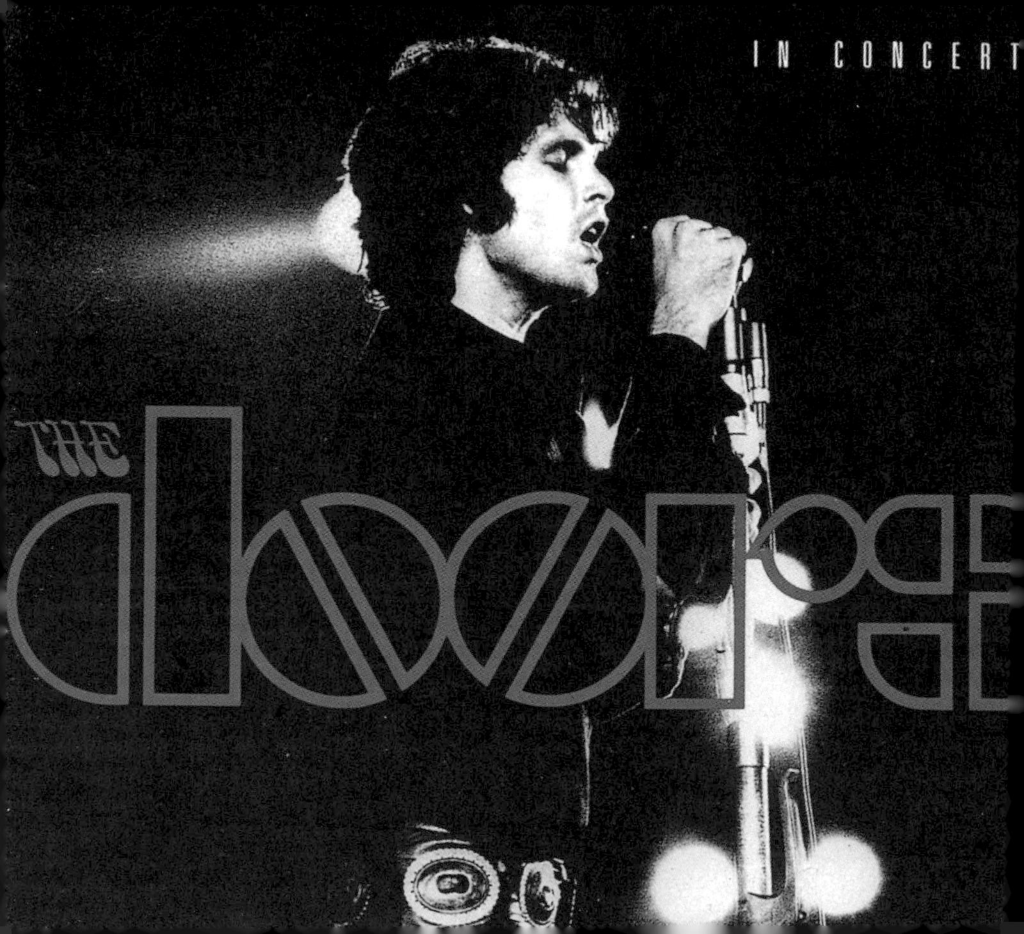
IN CONCERT
THE doors

The Later Live Albums

June 1980 saw the publication of No One Here Gets Out Alive, by Jerry Hopkins and Danny Sugerman. Hopkins had interviewed Morrison for *Rolling Stone* and had travelled to Mexico with The Doors; his first book, Elvis (which remains one of the best biographies of Presley published to date) had been dedicated in part to Jim Morrison "for the idea", and he commenced working on a book about The Doors shortly after Morrison's death. But his first draft of the book was rejected by over thirty different publishers – for being too lengthy, and too dry. At this point Danny Sugerman – who had been a "management associate" in The Doors' office in its heyday, while still only just in his teens – entered the picture. Sugerman worked extensively on Hopkins' manuscript, adding extra material (of dubious authenticity) pertaining to Morrison's sexual and drug activities, and generally upping the scandal quotient. This final version was snapped up by Warner Books (who had rejected the book twice before), and became a surprise best-seller. "I think Jim Morrison was a modern-day god. Oh hell, at least a lord," Sugerman wrote in his introduction, and the line between fact and legend got blurred from then on in; appealing to the romantically inclined, the myth the book traded on most heavily was the idea that Morrison might still be alive. Out there, somewhere. The authors even refer to Morrison's "alleged" death.

Though the book was a treasure trove of hitherto unknown and little-known facts, the groupie stories were more than a little distasteful to many readers (me included), and both the Morrison and Courson families went rushing to consult their lawyers.

Jac Holzman dismissed the book entirely: "The book was nothing but a repackaging job – not serious. It was too monumental, and tended to sensationalise aspects of Jim's character best ignored. The death rumours? Not only sick but unbelievable.

Danny Sugerman – how can I phrase this tactfully – wasn't as tight with Jim as you'd think from the book... I doubt if anyone knew Jim *that* well."

But the scandal angle undoubtedly caused the book's huge sales, got Hollywood talking about a possible Doors movie and consequently affected the way publishers viewed rock star biographies; doubtless it also encouraged Albert Goldman that the sleazy approach was just the ticket for shifting units – a trick he's since pulled on Elvis and John Lennon (he's now working on his own 'version' of the Morrison story).

Elektra capitalised on all the resultant media brouhaha by releasing yet another 'Greatest Hits' package, which ended up going platinum – while the band's entire back catalogue also suddenly started selling like hot cakes. Many of those buying were still in primary school when Jim died. Once again, his image was appearing on T-shirts and posters (and still is, to this day), and the books just kept on coming – at the time of writing (1993) there are over a dozen books on the shelves by or about Jim Morrison and The Doors.

A year after the Hopkins/Sugerman book first appeared, *Rolling Stone* ran a piece on the burgeoning Morrison industry. "He's Hot, He's Sexy, He's Dead" their headline proclaimed, commenting that Jim's appeal lay in the fact that the young always had need for "an idol who wasn't squeaky clean". Which Jim certainly wasn't. But that didn't stop the faithful from all over the world making pilgrimages to his Paris grave site as if he were a hipster saint. There they hung out, imbibing booze (and other substances) and toasting the Lizard King. At several times, the cemetery authorities and/or the police have felt the need to clear the area of admirers (when these include groups of mainlining junkies, one has to sympathise with the cemetery). Morrison's grave is impossible to miss – both his tombstone and the whole of the surrounding area are covered with so much graffiti that the scene looks more like the South Bronx than Paris, and the (hideous) bust of Jim which once decorated the site has long since been stolen by a souvenir-hunter. It's a pretty squalid resting place.

Naturally, with all this interest there was pressure on the surviving Doors to re-form on a more permanent basis. The group have so far wisely refused to do so – but though all have continued to work musically (without each other), none of these solo projects has yielded much significant fruit. And the cupboard, apparently, was bare of unreleased tapes.

That is, it was until footage of The Doors performing 'The WASP' and 'Love Me Two Times' on a Danish TV show in 1968 turned up. This prompted a hunt for other live tapes, which had vanished in the Seventies – they turned up in a Los Angeles storage warehouse. The tapes spanned a three-year period ('68-71), and both the surviving Doors and producer Paul Rothchild (reunited with the group for the first time since 1970) were determined not to repeat any of the material from 'Absolutely Live' (even if they came across better or more interesting versions) in their selection for possible release.

When eventually released in October 1983, the package was a mini-album titled 'Alive She Cried'. It finally made available a version of Van Morrison's 'Gloria' (a central showpiece for the group since their days at the Whiskey...) though unfortunately it was recorded at a soundcheck, and lacks the necessary audience response. Also of note are a version of Willie Dixon's 'Little Red Rooster', featuring John Sebastian on harmonica and some great slide guitar from Robbie, and a brooding, bluesy 'Moonlight Drive'. It was a worthy release, even if not totally 'authentic' – Krieger admitted the group had made some minor "improvements" to the tapes, and corrected the odd error.

Nor was this quite the end of legitimate Doors output. June 1987 saw the release of yet another live album, 'Live At The Hollywood Bowl'. Or perhaps it should be called a mini-album, since it has a total playing time of only nineteen minutes. Since four minutes of this had previously been released on 'Absolutely Live', the album wasn't exactly good value for money. On the plus side, it contained a stunning eight-minute version of 'Light My Fire'; on the downside, a promising version of 'Spanish Caravan' fades almost as soon as it starts (it clocks in at a mere one minute nineteen seconds). The whole project looked as if it had been put together without too much thought, leaving 'Alive She Cried' as undoubtedly the best of the three Doors' live albums.

'Hollywood Bowl' was released simultaneously on compact disc, an indication of the new format's growing popularity. All of The Doors' back catalogue – with two exceptions – is now available on CD, having been digitally remastered by Rothchild, Botnick and the surviving Doors. The exceptions are 'An American Prayer' (though not strictly speaking a Doors' album, it's still part of the canon... and still unreleased on CD at the time of writing) and 'Absolutely Live'. Rather than just do straight CD reissue of the latter, it was decided to compile *all* the Doors' live material on one CD set, under the title 'American Nights'. By the time the compilation was finally released in July 1991 the

title had been changed to the drearier 'In Concert', a double CD set which contained all the material from the three live albums (minus 'Spanish Caravan'), plus the version of 'Roadhouse Blues' from 'An American Prayer' and a previously unreleased version of 'The End' from the Hollywood Bowl.

But there's no doubt at all that a major factor in The Doors' latter-day popularity lies in the mystery surrounding Morrison's death. Many wanted to believe him still alive, doubtless still writing poetry and living a simple peasant life somewhere far, far away from prying eyes. *Had* he simply disappeared? Morrison had long admired the French poet Arthur Rimbaud (he was even known to sign autographs in that name), who had also turned his back on success and started life again elsewhere. Many of Jim's fans (old and new) wanted to believe it. He could have faked it, they argue – he was rich enough. And there's no denying the romantic allure of the idea – wouldn't it be great if he *had*? Then again, let's face it, there are still people out there who believe that James Dean,

Adolf Hitler and Amelia Earhart are alive.

One person for whom the question niggled unbearably was photo-journalist Bob Seymore. If only, Seymore thought, if only he could track down and photograph a living Jim Morrison, it would earn him a fortune and establish his career as an intrepid photo-sleuth. Of course, the first step in finding a living Morrison was to establish that Jim *wasn't* dead. As detailed in his book *The End* (Omnibus, 1991), Seymore journeyed to Paris and followed the trail as far as it would go, through mountains of red tape, and produced more concrete evidence (from Parisian police files) than any earlier researcher (there has never been any *official* inquiry into Jim's death).

Seymore's book explores the many oddities and unresolved questions surrounding Morrison's death; to prove the identity of the corpse, Pamela showed police Morrison's old passport. But his *current* passport has never been found. Why have his family and the other Doors left his body to lie in such a shoddy, miserable grave? (To be fair, the band did pay a large sum for the grave's upkeep... but somebody supposedly absconded with the money.) Why wasn't Pamela buried alongside Jim when she died? Who was the mysterious man who was "with Jim when he died" who telephoned Jim's editor Jonathan Dolger requesting the telegram Jim had sent Dolger the day before he died?

Seymore is convinced that there are several people who know more than they're saying, and that there has been *some* kind of a cover-up concerning the events of July 3, 1971. But, he thinks, this cover-up probably concerns Morrison's use of illegal drugs – that Jim's fatal heart-attack was in fact drug-related (the drug being cocaine, or possibly even heroin – which was far more fashionable in Paris than coke at the time. It's quite possible that Jim took heroin thinking it was coke, and his wasted body was unable to adjust to this one final overload of abuse).

"Maybe the whole myth about Jim Morrison still being alive was created deliberately in order to sustain interest in

The Doors and their music," he concludes. "It's an attractive myth and record companies have done far worse things to promote sales over the years. If someone asked me whether I thought Jim Morrison was still alive, I would say the odds in favour are only about 1%. That is because Pamela and the emergency services were the only people to see a body and its identification was made by Pam and with reference to an old passport. The police accepted this and had no reason not to. They took Pam at her word that it was Jim Morrison.

"I cannot see Pam and Jim going to great lengths to get a real corpse, though it is just about possible that a friend of theirs died in the apartment and they realised that this was just the opportunity to disappear for which Jim had been waiting. But this is just a fantasy – after all, if Jim wanted to get away from it all he could simply have retired and remained in France where he was not all that well known. That way he would not have had to break up with Pamela.

"Pamela's subsequent life also belies the idea that Jim was alive in hiding. She rapidly degenerated into heroin addiction, made a number of suicide attempts, including one occasion when she drove a truck straight into the clothes shop, Themis, that Jim bought for her before they went to France. On April 25, 1974, three years after Jim's death, she died in her Hollywood apartment of a heroin overdose, apparently unable to get over Jim's death, and unable to start a fresh life for herself. There was certainly no evidence that she sneaked away to visit him in hiding, and it is unlikely that she would have colluded in a move which would have resulted in the break-up of their relationship. In many ways, her subsequent life as a grieving widow is the greatest proof we have that Jim is dead."

These sentiments echo a statement made by Ray Manzarek in 1980: "If Pamela was any indication, then Jim was dead. She wasn't faking it. This was a woman who was totally broken up. Jim was her total life and she was devastated, so I assume Jim was dead from her reaction and the fact that the coffin was put into the ground, and that no one else has ever said otherwise. But... who knows?" Who knows, indeed? There's always that one per cent chance: if you really *want* to, you can still believe.

But Seymore wasn't the only person digging up facts in Paris in 1991. A film director named Oliver Stone had employed dozens of researchers to investigate every aspect of Jim's life there, as background material for his forthcoming film of Jim's life, to be titled simply *The Doors*. The shaman was coming home, to Hollywood.

(THE MOVIE AND SOUNDTRACK)

Though Jim Morrison's own cinematic aspirations had been headed in the general direction of art movies (Jean-Luc Godard, to be specific) his life story was pure, mainstream Hollywood. A hippie James Dean? It couldn't fail. Nevertheless, though Hollywood producer Sasha Harari bought the film rights to Hopkins' and Sugerman's No One Here Gets Out Alive in 1981, it took him the next ten years to actually get the film made. En route John Travolta, Richard Gere and Charlie Sheen expressed an interest in the starring role as Morrison, while Brian de Palma, Martin Scorcese, Ron Howard and Francis Ford Coppola were among the interested directors. Travolta was supposedly so keen on landing the role that he spent hours learning all Jim's stage moves (from videotapes supplied by The Doors themselves). The group were apparently so impressed that (unlikely as it may sound) they seriously considered taking to the road again, with Travolta as lead vocalist. According to Densmore, the idea was dropped because Travolta was just too "nice" to be convincing – he lacked Morrison's edge.

Early on, Harari contacted former Doors producer Paul Rothchild to ask him to produce the music for the film, feeling that his involvement – and that of the surviving Doors – was vital for the film's success. But The Doors themselves were not convinced that Harari would do right by the subject matter. As Rothchild recalls, "I had a call from Ray Manzarek who said, 'You're going to get a visit from the guy who has the option. Don't give him a break. Stonewall him.' So I did. Then Sasha kept calling and coming over to my house, and finally, after a couple of months, I called Ray back and said, 'Ray, this man has his heart in it. This man is full of passion. Let's open the door for him and see what happens.' And we did."

Manzarek and Jerry Hopkins collaborated on a tentative screenplay, but the project was to be stonewalled by legal problems. Jim's estate – including all uses of his writing – was now jointly controlled by the Morrison and Courson families (Jim had left Pamela everything, but she died without leaving a will; in 1979 a court action by the Morrison family contesting Jim's estate was settled with this joint arrangement – though as Jerry Hopkins points out, it's somewhat ironic that the use of Jim's writings is controlled by a retired High School principal and a retired admiral). The families refused to co-operate with any film – which wouldn't have made the project impossible, just very unlikely (Hollywood producers don't go out of their way to court lawsuits).

Apart from the problem with the Morrison and Courson families, two screenplays had been rejected and a third was delayed by a 6-month-long writers' strike, while the contract option for The Doors' co-operation lapsed and was renewed several times.

Despite all this, Harari and his co-producer Brian Glazer still somehow managed to secure the directorial talents of Oliver Stone, who was one of their top three choices (the other two were Martin Scorcese and Stanley Kubrick). Stone had begun discussions with them in 1986, and by 1989 was committed to the project, which he was to write and direct. The director of *Wall Street* and *Salvador*, Stone had won Oscars for his two studies of the Vietnam war, *Platoon* and *Born On The Fourth Of July*. He was a Vietnam vet himself, and a one-time drug-user; surely, if anyone could capture the spirit of Jim's music, life and times, Stone was the man.

By 1989 the Morrison estate had also finally (in return for an unspecified sum of money) agreed to the project, provided that the film contained no mention of other members of the Morrison family; the Coursons also agreed, provided that the film contained nothing linking Pamela detrimentally with Jim's death, and that the screenplay would not be based on *No One Here Gets Out Alive*, a book which they described as "a vile, despicable rip-off".

Stone's visual research – and the eventual physical 'look' of the film – was thorough to the point of obsession. Not only were buildings on Sunset Strip reconstructed back to their '67 heyday for a few brief seconds' worth of finished screen time, but even envelopes lying on desks in the background of domestic and office scenes bore the correct addresses! Stone's researchers tore LA and Paris apart in their search for material, and many witnesses turned up as extras (Patricia Kennealy appears in the film as a Wicca priestess, performing 'her' own wedding ceremony. Kennealy's book was supposedly a major reference work for Stone, though only John Densmore's book and Danny Sugerman's *Illustrated History* receive screen credits). Filming finally began in March 1990.

By then, of course, Stone had found his 'Jim' in Val Kilmer, a classically trained Californian actor whose most notable previous screen roles had been as Iceman, Tom Cruise's rival in *Top Gun*, and as the swashbuckling buffoon Madmartigan in Ron Howard's fairytale adventure *Willow* (during the filming of which Kilmer met his wife-to-be, actress Joanne Whalley). Whatever flaws Stone's film possesses (and there are many), the faults certainly don't lie in Val Kilmer's portrayal of Morrison – it's an *uncanny* impersonation.

Kilmer – who insisted on being called 'Jim' at all times while the movie was being shot – studied hours (days, more likely) worth of live Doors' tapes, and as many interview tapes of Jim speaking as he could lay his hands on, in order to capture Morrison's vocal inflections and nuances. One result of all this – against all expectations – was that Kilmer ended up supplying all his own vocals for the film – the only time that Morrison's vocals are heard is when Doors' records are playing in the background. For the concert scenes, Kilmer was wired with two earpieces, and as Rothchild recalls: "Val was hearing his own pre-recorded vocal, and he'd say, 'I'd like to hear Jim's vocal while I'm doing this. Sometimes he'd say, 'Give me Jim in the left ear and myself in the right ear'. Val is singing live on camera. It's a miracle. He's brilliant."

The vocal impersonation was a bonus, and not an aspect of the role that had figured much in Oliver Stone's thinking when

Kilmer was cast. "I'm sure when Oliver was thinking of the film, he never envisioned that as a possibility," Kilmer later commented. "But I managed to get close enough. What I'm proud of is that it's really hard to tell. I even fooled The Doors' road manager. I said, 'Is this New Orleans or Chicago or Rochester? I can't remember.' And it wasn't Morrison." The live material in the film is credited to The Doors "with additional vocals by Val Kilmer", though it's worth noting that none of these tracks was included on the soundtrack album.

If the vocal accuracy was uncanny, the physical presence Kilmer wielded when in character could be downright spooky. "On occasions I would turn around, look up, and Jim would be standing there," Rothchild later told Jane Garcia. "Val and I were in pre-production for several months, and as time went on and he more and more, as I called it, 'wore the mantle', I would sometimes in complete ease call him 'Jim'. That's how much he reminded me of him. Sometimes he'd be in the vocal booth recording, and he'd be in

Jim's position, holding things in a certain way and singing, and I'd look up and go, 'It's Jim.'" Jerry Hopkins describes a similar experience after spending an evening with Kilmer and Stone, and Bobby Krieger apparently thought Kilmer knew Morrison better than Jim knew himself.

But Kilmer certainly had no illusions about the character he was portraying. "It wasn't that much fun to be him because he really lived in pain – self-inflicted or born with it... But he was very impish, so that I related to him strongly. Very much an actor's spirit. That's another way of saying he was a schizophrenic. He was hardcore bonko. Also, he was striving for respect for, in many ways, a dead medium – poetry. That's something I've always been interested in, and I found it very easy to relate to the frustration of writing a bad poem." Kilmer had had a volume of his own poetry published, and knew something of Jim's experience in that area. "I know what it's like to write a bad poem and still be in love with the idea, but not get it across, and to be lost in that way.

"And he was so willing to damage and

destroy, as much as he inspired. A very challenging character, which I do respect. I don't respect that he felt the need to harm people. I think it's a lot harder to be yourself and yet be respectful of others. I don't think that was much on his agenda." And even after submerging himself so deeply in the role, Kilmer didn't fear he'd fall prey to Morrison's demons: "I don't have those same fights in me, so I'm not going to go into a bar and create them. I don't have any fear that will be my fate."

Not everyone was convinced by Kilmer's portrayal; writing in *Esquire*, Jim's former girlfriend Eve Babitz asked: "What can Val Kilmer know of being fat all of his life and suddenly one summer taking so much LSD and waking up a prince? Val Kilmer has always been a prince, so he can't have the glow, when you've never been a mudlark, it's just not the same."

But despite Kilmer's stunning enactment (or perhaps because it *is* so accurate), the finished film still makes for uneasy and depressing viewing. Stone concentrates on Morrison's degeneration, and what little we see of Jim's charm and talent is overshadowed by the decline into alcoholism and boorishness; the sexy rock star who drank too much, more than the counterculture icon. And watching Jim drink himself to death on the screen is no more fun than it can have been in real life.

Many thought Stone had also overplayed the sex angle. Meg Ryan (as Pamela) refused point blank to go through with one bedroom scene, and looks distinctly uncomfortable with the nudity aspect. (Ryan does her best in the role, but is saddled with the fact that the script reduces the Jim/Pamela relationship to 'I Love Lucy' status. "My part was meant to have been developed, and it just wasn't. It was a complete nothing," she later complained). Asked early on to summarise Stone's 'vision' of Morrison, Val Kilmer had admitted that it was "tits and acid". And tits there are aplenty: there's so much nudity in the concert sequences that you'd think it must have been obligatory to remove your clothing at the door.

After his film of Ron Kovic's autobiography *Born On The Fourth Of July* was

released, Stone was accused of fictionalising Kovic's account and admitted that he'd told "small lies in trying to reveal larger truths". Many (Kennealy and Manzarek, to name but two) felt that he'd used the same approach with Jim's story. But what "larger truths" was Stone trying to reveal here?

Whatever point Stone may have been trying to convey about Morrison and the turbulent times he lived in, it doesn't come across. The shaman angle is stressed throughout, starting with a scene of the dying Indian Jim supposedly witnessed as a child, and the character keeps appearing to Jim throughout the rest of the film (so often you imagine he must be playing Tonto to Morrison's Lone Ranger). Jim is hazily presented as a visionary (via muddied mysticism and Freudian tosh), an aspect which reaches its nadir in the sequence in which Morrison takes the other Doors out to the desert for a peyote trip. "I'll always be with you," Jim tells the others, in a Christ-allegory that's both clumsy and deeply pretentious. At least Stone spares us Jim's 'resurrection', and the bathtub scene (followed by a mawkish trip to Père Lachaise) is presented as what it almost certainly was: Jim's final curtain.

In a standard Hollywood biopic simplification, the other Doors are reduced to the status of mere ciphers, well-meaning but dumb compared to Morrison. Only Kyle McLachlan (special agent Dale Cooper from *Twin Peaks*) in an implausible blonde wig as Ray Manzarek really gets to *do* anything: whenever Kilmer/Jim says anything vaguely 'profound', McLachlan looks deeply thoughtful. Presumably he was meant to be Saint Peter.

On the plus side, besides Kilmer's performance, the film had two major success areas going for it: the camerawork, and the concert sequences (which really do capture the energy and excitement of The Doors live), both of which were stunning. But it still leaves you feeling cheated, and The Doors themselves must have felt the same way. Ray Manzarek hated Stone's script and refused to have anything to do with the film, while the other two had – at best – mixed feelings.

Regardless, the film – which was released in May 1991 – still managed to stoke the fires of the Morrison myth, and whether they liked it or not, the group would still profit by it. None of their solo ventures had fared that well, and – as we have seen – they had a vested interest in promoting The Doors' back catalogue: even *before* the film got off the ground, the surviving Doors were each earning over half a million dollars a year from their back catalogue. Not an inconsiderable sum, for what was effectively a pension; too bad Jim wasn't around to share it. As Krieger observed: "He's a legend, but he's dead and gone. You *can* make a mark on this life and be around to enjoy it. Learn from this."

Discography

This discography lists only original release details. Reissued singles are not included.

SINGLES

**Break On Through/
End Of The Night**
Elektra 45611 January 1967.

Light My Fire/The Crystal Ship
Elektra 45615 April 1967.

People Are Strange/Unhappy Girl
Elektra 45621 September 1967.

**Love Me Two Times/Moonlight
Drive**
Elektra 45624 November 1967.

**The Unknown Soldier/We Could
Be So Good Together**
Elektra 45628 March 1968.

Hello I Love You/Love Street
Elektra 45635 June 1968.

Touch Me/Wild Child
Elektra 45646 December 1968.

Wishful, Sinful/Who Scared You
Elektra 45656 February 1969.

Tell All The People/Easy Ride
Elektra 45663 May 1969.

Running Blue/Do It
Elektra 45675 August 69.

**You Make Me Real/Roadhouse
Blues**
Elektra 45685 March 1970.

**Love Her Madly/
Don't Go No Farther**
Elektra 45726 March 1971.

Riders On The Storm/Changeling
Elektra 45738 June 1971.

ALBUMS

THE DOORS

Break On Through (To The Other Side)/Soul
Kitchen/The Crystal Ship/Twentieth Century
Fox/Alabama Song (Whisky Bar)/Light My

Fire/Back Door Man/I Looked At You/End Of
The Night/Take It As It Comes/The End
Elektra 74007; CD 974 007-2 January 1967.

STRANGE DAYS

Strange Days/You're Lost Little Girl/Love Me
Two Times/Unhappy Girl/Horse
Latitudes/Moonlight Drive/People Are
Strange/My Eyes Have Seen You/I Can't See
Your Face In My Mind/When The Music's
Over
Elektra 74014; CD 974 014-2 October 1967

WAITING FOR THE SUN

Hello I Love You/Love Street/Not To Touch
The Earth/Summer's Almost Gone/Wintertime
Love/The Unknown Soldier/Spanish
Caravan/My Wild Love/We Could Be So
Good Together /Yes, The River Knows/
Five To One
Elcktra 74024; CD 974 024-2 July 1968

THE SOFT PARADE

Tell All The People/Touch Me/Shamans
Blues/Do It/Easy Ride/Wild Child/Runnin'
Blue/Wishful Sinful/The Soft Parade
Elektra 75005; CD 7559-75005-2 July 1969

MORRISON HOTEL

"Hard Rock Cafe" side: Roadhouse
Blues/Waiting For The Sun/You Make Me
Real /Peace Frog/Blue Sunday/
Ship Of Fools
"Morrison Hotel" side: Land Ho!/
The Spy/Queen Of The Highway/
Indian Summer /Maggie McGill
Elektra 75007; CD 975 007-2 February1970.

ABSOLUTELY LIVE

Who Do You Love/Alabama Song/Back Door
Man/Love Hides/Five To One/Build Me A
Woman/When The Music's Over/Close To
You/Universal Mind/Break On Through # 2/
The Celebration Of The Lizard/
Soul Kitchen
Elektra 2-9002 July 1970.

LA WOMAN

The Changeling/Love Her Madly/Been Down
So Long/Cars Hiss By My Window/L.A.
Woman/America/Hyacinth House/Crawling
King Snake/The Wasp (Texas Radio and the
Big Beat)/Riders On The Storm
Elektra 75011; CD 975 011-2 April 1971.

OTHER VOICES

Elektra K 42104; no CD release as of this
writing. *December 1971.*

FULL CIRCLE

Elektra 42116; no CD release as of this
writing. *September 1972.*

AN AMERICAN PRAYER

1) Awake/GhostSong/
Dawn's Highway/Newborn Awakening
2) To Come Of Age : Black Polished Chrome/
Latino Chrome Angels And Sailors/Stoned
Immaculate 3) The Poet's Dreams : The
Movie/Curses, Invocations 4) World On Fire:
AmericanNight/Roadhouse Blues/Lament/
The Hitchhiker 5) An American Prayer
This album is credited to: Jim Morrison, Music
by The Doors. It consists of a recording of Jim
Morrison reciting his "poems, lyrics and sto-
ries", over a musical backing from the three
surviving Doors, and features versions of The
Wasp and Riders On The Storm, a live version
of Roadhouse Blues, and new music especially
written and recorded for this album.
*Elektra 5E-502; no CD release as of this
writing November 1978.*

ALIVE, SHE CRIED

Gloria/Light My Fire/You Make Me Real/
Texas Radio & The Big Beat/Love Me Two
Times/Little Red Rooster/Moonlight Drive
*Elektra 96-0269-1; CD 060269-2
November 1983.*

LIVE AT THE HOLLYWOOD BOWL

Wake Up/Light My Fire/The Unknown
Soldier/Little Games/The Hill Dwellers/
Spanish Caravan
Elektra EKT 40; CD 960741 2 June 1987.

IN CONCERT

Who Do You Love/Alabama Song/Back
Door Man/Love Hides/Five To One/Build
Me A Woman/When The Music's Over/
Close To You/Universal Mind/Petition The
Lord With Prayer/Dead Cats, Dead
Rats/Break On Through # 2/The
Celebration Of The Lizard (Lions In The
Street/Wake Up/A Little Game /The Hill
Dwellers/Not To Touch The Earth/Names
Of The Kingdom/The Palace Of Exile)/
Soul Kitchen/Roadhouse Blues/Gloria/
Light My Fire (includes Graveyard

Poem)/You Make Me Real/Texas Radio
& The Big Beat/ Love Me Two
Times/Little Red Rooster/Moonlight
Drive (includes Horse Latitudes)/Close
To You/ Unknown Soldier/The End
Elektra CD 7559-61082-2 July 1991.

THE DOORS - MUSIC FROM THE ORIGINAL MOTION PICTURE

The Movie*/Riders On the Storm/Love
Street/Break On Through/The End/Light
My Fire/Ghost Song*/Roadhouse Blues/
Heroin - performed by The Velvet Under-
ground & Nico/Carmina Burana, per-
formed by the Atlanta Symphony Orch-
estra and Chorus, conducted by Robert
Shaw/Stoned Immaculate*/ When The
Music's Over/The Severed Garden
(Adagio)*/L.A. Woman
Elektra CD 7559-61047-2 May 1991.
Tracks marked * are extracts from the An
American Prayer album, performed by Jim
Morrison and The Doors. All other tracks
(unless otherwise indicated) are per-
formed by The Doors, and are the original
album versions with vocals by Jim
Morrison, *not* Val Kilmer.

Anthologies

THE BEST OF THE DOORS

Break On Through/Light My Fire/The
Crystal Ship/People Are Strange/
Strange Days/Love Me Two Times/
Alabama Song/Five To One/Waiting For
The Sun/Spanish Caravan/When The
Music's Over/Hello, I Love You/
Roadhouse Blues/L.A. Woman/Riders
On The Storm/Touch Me/Love Her
Madly/Unknown Soldier/The End
Elektra CD 7559-60345-2 November 1985.

Numerous other 'best of' anthologies
have been released over the years, some
of them shoddily put together (like the hit
single-biased '13'), some of them more
thoughtfully constructed to give a better
perspective on the group's career (such
as Weird Scenes Inside The Goldmine,
which wins the best title award, if nothing
else). None of them contain any material
unavailable elsewhere, as all of them bar
the current Best Of The Doors listed
above have long since been deleted.

her voices, full circle
& an American Prayer

Other voices, full circle
& an American Prayer

L.A.

Strange Days

The surviving Doors with Pearl Jam's Eddie Vedder at the Rock and Roll Hall of Fame.